THE S/B

STOCK MARKET RATIO

PROFITING FROM LEGAL INSIDER TRADING

Edwin A. Buck

New York Institute of Finance

Library of Congress Cataloging-in-Publication Data

Buck, Edwin A.
  The S/B stock market ratio.

  Includes index.
    1. Investments—United States. 2. Stocks—United States. 3. Insider
trading in securities—United States. I. Title.
HG4910.B82 1988   332.63'22   87-31500
ISBN 0-13-785643-1

*

This publication is designed to provide accurate and authoritative information in regard to the subject matter covered. It is sold with the understanding that the publisher is not engaged in rendering legal, accounting, or other professional service. If legal advice or other expert assistance is required, the services of a competent professional person should be sought.

From a Declaration of Principles Jointly Adopted by
a Committee of the American Bar Association and a
Committee of Publishers and Associations

Printed in the United States of America

10 9 8 7 6 5 4 3 2 1

New York Institute of Finance
(NYIF Corp.)
70 Pine Street
New York, New York 10270-0003

Dedicated to my crew: Joan B. Buck and Maria Gisondi.

Contents

Preface

The analytical tool that is perhaps most used by investors and financial professionals is the price:earnings (P/E) ratio. It is the bottom line, the summation of a company's success or lack of success, and the measure by which Wall Street evaluates, or is willing to pay for, a company's earnings.

This book introduces a new ratio and attempts to prove that it at least approaches in value the esteemed P/E ratio. The new ratio is the sell:buy (S/B) ratio, which is the number of sales compared to the number of buys effected by those most knowledgeable of investors: *the corporate insiders*. The S/B ratio is the summation of what thousands of executives think about the value of their companies.

The S/B ratio should also be valued for its predictive character. The following pages present a solid case to show that collectively the insiders, having distilled all the factors that are shaping and will shape the future of their companies, can give us a way to maximize our investment results by conquering that all-important but elusive investment dilemma: *timing*. This claim cannot be made for the P/E ratio.

Market forecasts shaped by insider activity that have been chronicled and published by me include the following:

- December 2, 1974, Dow 598: "Unusual... more insiders buying than selling." In May 1975, the Dow reached 859 (+44%).
- April 14, June 30, and July 21, 1982, Dow 790/830: "Unusual... more insiders buying than selling." The present bull market exploded in August and by February 1983, the Dow was 1135 (+35%).
- October 16, 1985, Dow 1369: "Insider buying is improving dramatically at a time the market is flirting with an all-time high—not an usual situation." In April 1986, the Dow was 1848 (+35%).
- October 29, 1986, Dow 1783: "Insiders are conducting a harmonious bull market adagio." In December 1986, the Dow reached 1956 (+10%).
- January 7, 1987, Dow 1950: "The stock market is still undervalued, and the Dow should see at least 2750 during 1987." In February 1987, the Dow was 2201 (+13%), and on August 27, 1987, the Dow reached an intraday reading of 2756 (+39%).

By learning to use the sell:buy ratio, J. Q. Investor will now be better equipped to handle a quixotic market. Whether an investor studies insider activity to pick stocks and then applies basic research, or chooses selections by means of the usual analytical techniques and then "confirms" those selections by checking them with those of the insiders, the S/B ratio can be a valuable tool.

After the Crash

The Insiders' Trading Formula guided us through the bull market with great success. But Monster Monday, October 19, 1987, posed the greatest test for anyone's market theory, including that proposed in this book. Could it cope with a two-week historic bear market? Yes it did, with an excellent grade.

On September 23, 1987 I wrote that the S/B ratio had weakened for nine consecutive weeks and, because of this trend, we were not going to wait for an actual reading of 2.5 — "we are fixing our stop-loss on stocks this week . . . because the market also is weakening, the stops are quite tight (near present prices).'' And on September 30: ''The eight-week S/B is almost at a mandatory 'no buy' of 2.50.''

These stops started being executed on October 9, 1987, and by the morning of October 19 we were out of all our stopped stocks. GLENFED was retained because we calculated the stock was selling at only two times 1988 earnings. BRT Realty was also kept since the stock was yielding 15%! We doubled our position in the latter on Tuesday, October 20. The company increased its dividend each of the last five quarters and had a book value of almost $15 per share. We are willing to sit with that till "what-you-call-it" freezes over.

Refer to the Insiders' Portfolio's first "annual report" (pages 144 and 145). On that date, October 5, 1987, the portfolio was worth 44% more than at its inception (with no fresh funds invested).

After the carnage on Monster Monday, the Insiders' Portfolio had $21,088 in stock and $35,748 in valuable cash. Although our 44% was pared to 14%, we escaped a good deal of potential loss. If we had not put stop-loss orders (see Chapter 4) on 8 of our 10 stocks, we would have held stocks with a value of $39,238 — a loss of 22% — *with no cash to reinvest.*

The Insiders' Trading Formula was conceived with a primary objective of capital preservation. And it performed well. Also, one advantage of a crash is that it affords investors an opportunity to reshuffle, reorganize, upgrade, and shed themselves of mistakes. The good value equities are hit as hard as the lesser quality issues, especially in the recent blue-chip boom and bust brought on by foreign investors.

Earlier selling in 1987 would have meant that tremendous price increases would not have been realized. Holding through the Crash would have meant that we would have no cash to take advantage of cheap prices.

Our first new acquisition for the Insiders' Portfolio was Coca-Cola at 33½. By October 30, the stock sold at 43! Coke had an insider rating of +40 — very high for a blue chip. NCR, the next new insertion, was purchased on October 28 at 53 as the stock (bashed from a year's high of 87) not only operationally is performing in a sterling manner, but has the highest insider office equipment rating. Only three closings later, the stock ended the day at 63¼!

These purchases were affected not because we were nimble and daring traders, but because the S/B dramatically improved after the Crash from over 3.00 readings in September to under our buy point of 1.5. Stops will be placed to protect us from a possible recurrence of the Crash, and leave us with noteworthy gains.

1

Who Are the Insiders?

As this book is being written, much ado (about nothing?) is going on about the activities of certain outsiders who are called insiders by the Securities and Exchange Commission—investment bankers, proxy printers, lawyers, and so on. But the *true* insider is an officer or a director or a large stockholder (at least 10%) of a corporation. The real insider is an employee or an affiliate of the company who holds a position at the executive level or whose involvement in corporate affairs is at a comparably high level.

The true insider legally possesses inside information because it is his or her job to *know*, to ferret out, all the information that can possibly aid or hinder the company in enhancing its bottom line. This person is the insider who is going to help us to vastly increase the bottom line of our investments.

It is simplistic to say that a company's officers know their company better than any outsider does. Yet this obvious truism has been mostly overlooked by Wall Street, investment advisers, and money managers. Wall Street analysts try to keep their contacts with corporate officers open at all times, but the analysts pay attention only to what their contacts say and neglect what is more important—what they *do*. What they do can often differ from what they say.

We are going not only to see what corporate officers and affiliates are doing, but by using certain techniques, we will learn to ascertain *why* they are doing what they are doing. The "why" is most important. Many trades are undertaken for reasons having nothing to do with investments. We are going to learn how to dissect insiders' activities so that we will be almost categorically able to say: "That trade (or those trades) was an investment decision, and we should pay attention."

Insider Activity and Security Analysis

The dictionary defines an insider as "one who is within a limited circle of persons who understand the actual facts in a case." It is our job to persistently search for the actual facts by analyzing insiders' actions. I will prove that insider activity should take a foremost position in security analysis.

- From May 22 to July 9, 1986, eight insiders sold 182,992 shares of Floating Point. In July, the company reported the first quarterly earnings decrease in seven years. The market price dropped from $33.50 to $19 in just a few days.

- Emerging in April 1978, as a spin-off from a bankruptcy, but destined to revolutionize the giant toy industry under the able aegis of Charles Lazarus, Toys 'R' Us made early investors wealthy shareholders. Earnings rose from 16¢ a share to 93¢ by 1984. Throughout this period, corporate officers repeatedly bought in the open market. Suddenly, in the late summer of 1984, these officers seemed to change their minds. By September, with the stock at $50, 10 officers had sold 223,730 shares. In December, the company announced that Christmas sales would be a disappointment. In a matter of days, the stock tumbled 11 points.

- Private hospital stocks were the bright lights of Wall Street during 1983 and 1984. Almost all of them enjoyed hefty increases in share price—100% by many. During this period, however, corporate officers did not seem to agree with Wall Street; they were continual and heavy sellers. From July to September 1985, 10 officers of Hospital Corporation of America sold 101,413 shares. There were no buys by officers. Then in early October, at a meeting with Wall Street analysts, the chairman of the corporation announced that foreseeable earnings would be flat. Next day, the stock fell 7¾ points. Most other hospital stock prices were slashed by sizable amounts in reaction to what had happened to Hospital Corporation of America.

- Coleco Industries made a bunch from the Cabbage Patch dolls and, with new accessories for them, was looking forward to a merry 1985 Christmas. In August, however, amid protestations that the sales were to raise cash for option exercises, six officers sold 194,800 shares at prices ranging from $18.25 to $16. In January the company announced that it expected a fourth quarter decline in earnings of about 35%. The stock fell from $20 to $10 by September.

- After OPEC seized control of the oil market and raised prices 900%, oil stocks went through the roof—particularly the stock of the smaller producers. In the face of increasingly bullish pronouncements from Wall Street, oil company insiders sold their stocks as if solar energy were around the corner. It wasn't—but they foresaw the oil glut that would cause their stocks to plunge even faster than they had gone up. Conversely, oil industry officers were on the buy side when the low of $9 a barrel was reached late in 1986, and soon after, the oil stocks appreciated about 25%—much more than the Dow.

- When Judge Green ruled for the divestiture of AT&T, much concern, anxiety, and doubt arose in the minds of investors. Ma Bell's stock soon dipped to $17 from the mid-20s. The regional Bell stocks left the gate limping. Yet, throughout 1984 and 1985 they were stellar performers. The next two years witnessed 37 corporate insiders buying and *only one* selling. Each Baby Bell stock appreciated 50% or more. AT&T sold at $36 a share by August 1987.

- Daisy Systems announced on January 16, 1986, that it "agreed" with some analysts that quarterly earnings would drop around 35%. The stock dipped 5½ points in two days. Previously, in the final quarter of 1985, four insiders had sold 301,346 shares.

- The *Wall Street Journal* (January 17, 1986) "Micron Technology...is a fallen star—Will glory days come again?" Nine insiders the previous month had sold 915,000 shares in a range of $7.50 to $9.50 a share. The end of 1986 saw the stock trading at about $3 a share.

- Alliant Computer stock fell 7½ points on July 6, 1987, after the company reported that its second quarter earnings should see a 40% drop from the first quarter. Between May 8 and May 15 four insiders had sold 85,000 shares.

There are many, even hundreds, of other examples just as startling, but space prohibits a complete report. The foregoing examples, however, are sufficient to show that insiders can warn us of impending good or bad news.

Although the law reads that insiders cannot act on information that only they know, it is almost impossible to point an accusing finger except at definite events—a new development or a transaction predicated on news releases soon to be distributed. All else is in a gray area, and insiders can act on their knowledge and feelings. It is sometimes apparent that they do act on hard information. Such was the case when eight officers of Wang Laboratories sold 111,528 shares during the first quarter of 1985 shortly before the company reported lower earnings for the first time in more than three years. The stock's price shrank from $30 to $15 by mid-1985 and has yet to recover.

To obtain an edge over other investors, particularly other arbitrageurs, Ivan Boesky trespassed over the line of legality and lost his reputation, company, and possibly his freedom by clearly violating insider regulations. There is a legal way for any investor to obtain the edge, however, and that is by carefully noting and studying what the insiders are doing. This book will show that you can profit by accessing insider information in a sound and legal manner. There are several sources of insider information that will be described later.

It is pleasant and profitable to purchase a winning stock early and ride with it to loftier price levels as more and more investors are attracted to it. This book, too, will prove profitable because it promulgates investment techniques that most investors ignore or have not even heard of. This is to our advantage, for if the world employs the same method, the method loses its value— it no longer can be predictive. In one way, I hope that not every investor will read this book!

Assessing a Company's Present Status

When considering a company to work for or when selecting one for an important business contract, you naturally want to do more than just read what may be available about it. It is important to talk to and evaluate the company's executives. You should interview employees to ascertain morale, working conditions, and efficiency. So it is with investing. No annual report can (or wants to?) convey to you the absolute position that that company occupies—its weaknesses as well as strengths. By studying the actions of a company's officers (i.e., insiders), however, you can see how they are voting on their own prospects. If they are buying their company's stock on the open market, that is a big vote of confidence. A flurry of sales, on the other hand, is like the flashing of the yellow cautionary signal. The axiom that "action speaks louder than words" is a cornerstone of our insider theories.

Yesterday's financial figures may be impressive and can be indicative of tomorrow's—but not necessarily so. There are factors that only management may be aware of. The only complete and accurate assessment that can be made by us outsiders is of the past. True, if a company has successfully dealt with its previous challenges and opportunties, it would seem that it could do so now and in the future. The word "seem" is the important one. That is what investment is all about. Successful investing is latching on to the good "seems" and converting them to definitive future performance. When the "seems" become reality, we profit.

It is hard enough to evaluate all the yardsticks used in investments analysis: price:earnings ratios, price:sales ratios, return on capital, current ratio, yield, earnings as a percentage of sales, book value, and on and on. Yet all these yardsticks pertain to the present or to the past. If evaluation of them proves positive, we have a good "seems that."

Assessing a Company's Future

Successful investing depends on the future, however. And this is where the calculator, graph paper, and eraser leave off. We have to go beyond the relative safety of objectivity and we are forced to become subjective! We have arrayed our facts, but now we have to formulate our opinion.

There are as many tools proposed to help us to form an opinion as there are yardsticks in objective research. Foremost is the assumption that if the past and present look superlative, then a rosy future can be assumed. Maybe—but naive.

Chartists believe that future stock activity can be ascertained by stock trading patterns witnessed in the past. Again, naive.

Contrary investors look for stocks with unwarranted low prices or for those that having stumbled could regain their footing and give a run for their money. Without some hard indications, such opinions are merely presumptions.

Some investors patiently wait for a bear market so that they can buy blue chips that will, they hope, rise with the tide. Only luck will identify the low point of a market, and very often the bellwethers of a new bull market will not be those stocks that performed well before the shakedown. In fact, many new bull markets are set in motion with a change of leadership.

The best way to arrive at correct opinions and profitable investments is by studiously learning everything possible—and this means *everything* and combining this with years of experience and an uncommon common sense.

If you cannot devote the necessary hours to learning *everything* and possess merely average perspicuity, however, then this book will give you a method you *can* employ that should lead to successful investing and give you "tomorrow's news today." *And this will be proven!*

2

Reports Required of Insiders

I ended Chapter 1 by saying that I will *prove* that this book will give you a method for successful investing and for learning tomorrow's news today. That's a powerful statement, but it is fully justified. I have been tallying insider transactions every day since 1970, and insiders have shown me certain ways to decipher their actions and to divert their knowledge and experience to my own investment advantage.

It can be presumed that each insider does have more information about his company than it is possible for any outside investor to have. A collective study of *all* insider activity in *all*

ies should (and does) furnish us a lead time—even over
_ prescient stock market itself, the stock market that the
government says is their best "leading indicator."

My partner and I formerly ran a successful information
bureau in New York City, and our *Weekly Insider Report* was only
a small part of the business. Since selling our company to Argus
Research Corporation, I have had more time to expand theories
that were on the back burner in my mind, time to toss tangents
around and to conduct studies to prove my main contention,
which is that insiders can be of paramount importance to
successful investing. The more salient studies are reflected in this
book. First, though, I must stress an important characteristic of
my studies: Each study encompassed *all* stocks with certain
common characteristics. *All* had an index rating (to be explained
later) within the *same* range at the *same* time, or *each* was in my
"Top Ten" at the same time, *all* reversals were in the same time
frame, and so on. There has been no picking or choosing to prove
a point.

Mostly, I use the Dow Industrial Average as the control.
Perhaps the S&P 500 or the Wilshire Index (which has the most
stocks), would be better. Most people, however, relate to the Dow.
They know the trouble the Dow had for two decades in breaking
through 1000. Most can tell you the Dow's recent high and low.
Not so with the other indexes.

Form 4

Fortunately, it is easy to track what the insiders are doing.
The Investment Act of 1933 decreed that insiders file with the
Securities and Exchange Commission (SEC) a report (Form 4) on
all their transactions whether they be open market trades, awards,
or options. These forms 4 are filed with the exchanges on which
the stock is listed, as well as with the SEC. I go to both the
exchange and the SEC because for some reason (loss, the insider's
failure to file, and yes, unfortunately, theft) the SEC will often
have a form that the exchange does not (and vice versa).

The main reason the government wants Form 4 filed is to prevent insiders from buying or selling on the basis of information that is privy to them, information that for business reasons cannot be or has not been released for public dissemination. The government believes that it is wrong for the insider to act on information that has not been made public. Later on, I will show that this restriction does far more harm to the individual investor that if no regulation existed—especially if accurate and prompt filing of Form 4 is enforced. The regulation preempts an efficient market.

The following completed forms (as well as the Form 4) are available to the public at the SEC reference room or by writing to 450 5th Street, NW, Washington, DC 20001. Investors should know their nomenclature and descriptions. Forms marked with an asterisk are available at the Chicago and New York regional offices: 219 South Dearborn, #1204, Chicago, IL 60604; and 26 Federal Plaza, New York, NY 10278.

- *Form 10K.* A company's annual report to the SEC. It is more replete than the annual report sent to stockholders. Most companies will supply a copy of Form 10K upon request and must comply with any stockholder's request for a copy.
- *Form 10Q.* A company's quarterly report to the SEC.
- *Form 8-K.* A special report required to be submitted 10 days after a new material event to the company occurs.
- *Form 144.* A preliminary notice by insiders and/or holders of unregistered stock that they *intend* to sell. Requires name, address, shares to be sold, and intended broker.
- *Schedule 13D.* Any buyer who obtains 5% of any class of equity of a company must report this to the SEC. Schedule 13D has to be filed within 10 days of the purchase and declare the reason for the purchase—investment, potential proxy fight, potential acquisition, and so forth. Also, whenever the acquirer's holdings or purposes change, an amendment must be filed. (Vickers publishes a list of Forms 144 and Schedules 13D twice weekly.)

11

FIGURE 2–1a.

FORM 4

OMB APPROVAL
OMB Number: 3235-0287
Expires: January 31, 1989

U.S. SECURITIES & EXCHANGE COMMISSION
Washington, D.C. 20549

Statement of Changes in Beneficial Ownership of Securities

Filed pursuant to Section 16(a) of the Securities Exchange Act of 1934, Section 17(a) of the
Public Utility Holding Company Act of 1935 or Section 30(f) of the Investment Company Act of 1940

(Please print or type.)

1. NAME AND BUSINESS ADDRESS OF REPORTING PERSON

LAST   FIRST   MIDDLE

(ZIP CODE)

2. STATE OF INCORPORATION

3. IF AN AMENDMENT GIVE DATE OF STATEMENT AMENDED
MO.   DAY   YR.

4. NAME OF COMPANY

5. IRS OR SS IDENTIFYING NUMBER OF REPORTING PERSON

6. STATEMENT FOR CALENDAR MONTH OF
MONTH   YEAR

7. DATE OF LAST PREVIOUS STATEMENT
MO.   DAY   YR.

8. RELATIONSHIPS OF REPORTING PERSON TO COMPANY
(Instruction 3)

TABLE I. Securities Bought, Sold or Otherwise Acquired or Disposed of

Furnish the information required by the following table as to securities of the company bought or sold
or otherwise acquired or disposed of by the reporting person during the month for which this statement is
filed *(See Instruction 5)* and as to securities of the company beneficially owned, directly or indirectly, at the
end of the month. However, transaction involving the acquisition or disposition of puts, calls, options or
other rights or obligations to buy or sell securities of the company shall be reported in Table II.

1. TITLE OF SECURITIES *(Instruction 8)*	2. *(FOR SEC USE ONLY)*	3. DATE OF TRANSACTION *(Instruction 9)*	4. AMOUNT OF SECURITIES ACQUIRED *(Instruction 10)*	5. AMOUNT OF SECURITIES DISPOSED OF *(Instruction 10)*	6. CHARACTER OF TRANSACTION REPORTED *(Instruction 10)*	7. PURCHASE OR SALE PRICE PER SHARE OR OTHER UNIT *(Instruction 11)*	8. AMOUNT OWNED AT END OF MONTH *(Instruction 10)*	9. NATURE OF OWNERSHIP OF SECURITIES OWNED AT END OF MONTH *(Instruction 11)*

12

If during the month for which this statement is filed the reporting person acquired or disposed of any put, call, option or other right or obligation (all hereinafter referred to as "options") to buy or sell, or be required to buy or sell, securities of the company, furnish the information required by the following table. (*See Instruction 5*) However, the acquisition or disposition of transferable warrants issued by the company are to be reported in Table I. Options exempted by Rule 16a–6 need not be reported.

1. TITLE OF SECURITIES SUBJECT TO OPTION (*Instruction 8*)	2. (*FOR SEC USE ONLY*)	3. DATE OF TRANSACTION (*Instruction 9*)	4. NATURE OF OPTION (*Instruction 15*)	5. AMOUNT OF SECURITIES SUBJECT TO OPTION (*Instruction 10*)	6. CHARACTER OF TRANSACTION, IF ANY, REPORTED (*Instruction 12*)	7. PURCHASE OR SALE PRICE OF SECURITIES SUBJECT TO OPTION (*Instruction 11*)	8. DATE OF EXPIRATION OF OPTION

Explanation of items in tables:

DATE OF STATEMENT

SIGNATURE OF REPORTING PERSON

NOTE: *If the space provided in either table is insufficient, use a continuation sheet which identifies the table and columns to which it relates.*

- *Schedule 13G*. Filed by financial institutions that have a passive, normal course-of-business reason for stock purchase. Schedule 13G is filed in lieu of Schedule 13D.

- *Schedule 13F.* Institutions with portfolios that equal $100 million in value must file this form quarterly, outlining their portfolio and any changes that have occurred during the quarter. (Vickers publishes a quarterly report of all 13Fs and other "non–13F" institutions.)

Form 4 requires the insider not only to report his transaction but to reveal other information imperative to our analysis of his trade: his current holdings, office held, date, price, size of the trade, and most important, whether the transaction was consummated on the open market. We should look only at open market transactions because any other ownership changes, such as gifts or the exercise of options and dividends, are not investment decisions.

3

The Importance of Timing

Any investment method, be it long-term or short-term, needs to generate two ingredients:

1. *Confidence* that adequate groundwork has been undertaken (we have correctly analyzed the clues insiders have furnished).

2. *Patience* while we wait for the market to recognize our hypothesis.

The procedures I present in this book are not contingent on any theory or on an abstract mathematical formula. The technique is simply to employ the end result of the collective intelligence of thousands of the best-informed investors—the nation's corporate officers. They are the insiders who will help us outsiders make our investment decisions about selection and timing.

Basic Investment Decisions

Three fundamental decisions must be made in investing:

1. When to buy.
2. What to buy.
3. When to sell.

We will touch on the "what" by rating stocks according to insider activity. Two of the three decisions concern "when," however. Thus, timing is twice as important as selection.

By being wrong in timing, by being either lulled or panicked, an investor could have had disastrous results even if investing in only such long-term stalwarts as IBM or MMM. Likewise, an investor could have had good results by investing in mediocre stocks if his timing was good. Most stocks go up or down in unison. Of course, good selection and good timing are ideal. By the time you have reached the end of this book, I believe you will be better equipped to handle both.

When the market moves, it usually does so only in spurts. Moves of 10% over the past 20 years have occurred in only 65 months out of 240.

During periods of consolidation or apathy, when the market is listless, investors are wary of the next direction it will take. "Experts" abound who tell us it will collapse—or boom. When the market is moving decisively, about 25% of the time, most investors feel uncertain as to the extent or the timing of the move.

If we could reduce our risk by exiting the market when it is doing nothing, and then re-entering before losing too much on the upside, that would be super. If we could exit before a prolonged drop to take advantage of lower prices and then come realistically close to recognizing a market bottom, that would be even better.

And we can—by following America's myriad corporate managers. And why not? They orchestrate the economy. It is for us only to listen.

Some Recent History

Since 1973, the stock market has swung widely and its pendulum nature has caused either investor euphoria or gloom. For the first 10 of these years, the Dow Jones industrials gyrated at least 200 points—a whopping percentage in the 1970s. Now it can, and does, do this in a day or two.

In August 1974, the Dow crumpled almost 150 points. The next month the collapse continued when almost 100 additional points were lost. At the beginning of 1975 the Dow was at 900. By the end of September, it was below 600. Relative calm prevailed in 1976, which was a breather for investors; the Dow flirted with 1000 all year. It could not penetrate that barrier, however, and fell to 800 in 1977.

Both in October 1978 and a year later in October 1979 the Dow plunged 100 points—from 900 to 800. These were the "October Massacres." A few quotations from the *Wall Street Journal* and other sources of the time illustrate the prevailing doom and gloom. A glance at the charts on pages 28 to 31 shows clearly that the insiders were, like the market, unsettled at the time. However, they regrouped, bought into a collapsing market as they do when economics do not match the market's disarray, and as usual were proved right. The market soon improved. By following the insiders (the S/B ratio), traders would have pocketed a tidy profit.

- The *Wall Street Journal*, October 30, 1978: "A rapid rebound from the stock market's recent shattering down turn appears *unlikely* to some investment officers."

- The same issue headlined: "Analyst Believes Replay of 1974–75 Recession Would Cause 200–Point Plunge in Industrials."

- A former chairman of the President's Economic Advisors: "If the drop in the stock market doesn't stabilize...this would heighten the probabilities of a recession in 1979 *rather than 1980.*" (italics mine)

- Economist at Federated Research Corporation: "We believe the segmented bear market of the past one and a half years is over and that all sectors will be synchronized on the *downside.*" (italics mine)

- The *Wall Street Journal*, October 10, 1979: "Busiest day *ever.* Market dropped 8.27 points on 86 million shares." (Today 230 million shares is common.) (italics mine)

- The *Wall Street Journal*, October 12, 1979: "The market is like a man who has had a bad heart attack. It has suffered tremendous internal damage that will take a long time to repair."

- A money manager: "This [sell off] is likely to be just the opening salvo in a larger decline."

By the end of the year, the market had recovered.

In September 1985, I was quoted by the *Wall Street Journal* as predicting "a hell of a good market." This quotation was stimulated by an unusual, even unique, occurrence—insiders turned from selling to buying while the market was floundering around at all-time-high readings (see Figure 4–4 on page 31). To have the contrarian insiders begin buying close to a market top meant only one thing: The market had a long way to go on the upside. Indeed it did. To the tune of 250 points in three months!

In April 1981, for the third time since 1972, the Dow brushed against the magical 1000 only to be swept away and end 15 months later at 800. This caused pundits and gurus to predict an immediate collapse to 700 or 600, or even below. Instead, midway in 1982, the market abruptly turned, and one of the biggest and longest of bull markets ensued.

The 10 years from 1973 to 1983 were a period of traumatic happenings and changes for this country. Investors became confused and frustrated, and they left the market in droves. It began with Watergate. Inflation was rampant, greatly exceeding growth in personal income. Interest rates began their ascent with short-term rates exceeding long-term rates from 1978 to 1981 (a phenomenon that economists claim predicts imminent disaster). Both short- and long-term U.S. Treasury securities paid more than 13% in 1981.

Industry would not be able to function long with that high cost of money! Unemployment figures were bad and getting worse. The country realized that its treasures were finite. Infrastructure was crumbling. Japanese imports first threatened basic industry and then high technology. And the national debt!

As if this was not enough, the stock market itself changed to the detriment of individual investors. Institutions replaced individuals as the predominant player. When this happened, it was thought that the pros would be a stabilizing factor. However, institutions proved to be more lemming-like than the public. The competition for quarterly results replaced the steadier logic of long-term planning. Woe be it to the money manager whose quarterly report revealed inferior performance—regardless of the reason. As a result, money managers became hung up on a short-term hit-parade syndrome. A rush into stocks or a single stock often has been followed by a mass exodus. The resultant wide swings in prices causes consternation in the minds of individual investors.

For years only a few institutions, to say nothing of individuals, were able to match the performance of the averages. In

19

1983, the Standard & Poor 500 beat 73% of all investment managers. In 1984, it outperformed 69% of them. The professionals did little better in 1985 and in 1986. One thousand common stock pension and institutional funds showed a 10-year return of 14% compared to the S&P 500 of 13.8%. From 1981 to 1986, the S&P 500 outperformed these funds by almost 2%.

The Effects of Investment Innovations

Because of the vagaries of the stock market, the random walk became popular. Research and acumen could be replaced by throwing darts at the stocktables for investment selection. Many institutions gave up by resorting to portfolios of the indexes—little Dows or S&P 500s.

Another innovation has been the creation of specialized funds investing in gold, high tech, medical technology, or any other particular industrial category—with hope that the market would swing that way. Alas, investors were allowed to change from one fund to another in the same "family"—probably buying high and selling low at each switch!

Institutions are using a new technique of hedging by purchasing of index futures and then arbitraging between them and the mass sale or purchase of stocks. This practice leads to further distortions in the market. The New York Stock Exchange has estimated that as much as 30% of its total volume can be connected to options and futures. The much-feared "triple witching hour" occurs when four (yes, four) major indexes mature on the third Friday of the last month of each quarter, causing tremendous volume and perhaps price distortion. They are the S&P 500, the NYSE Composite, the Major Market Index, and the *Value Line*.

The surge of merger and acquisition activity plus anticipation of them causes further sharp increases and decreases in stock prices. The individual has learned that one unsuccessful deal can wipe out the profits of several successes.

All these stratagems and strivings by corporations, institutions, and other big-time operators contribute to the feeling of helplessness that now engulfs the individual investor. How can the individual cope with all these machinations? Many cannot.

FIGURE 3–1.

How the Individual Can Survive

This book proposes methods and techniques that will lead to a more sober viewpoint and keep the individual investor from being lulled or panicked into bad investment decisions. In fact, I will show that you will look forward to wide swings because you will be able to maximize your profits. Your employment of the techniques to be discussed will go a long way to even the score for you as an individual investor.

4

The S/B: How Many Sales? How Many Buys?

The cornerstone of our studies is the sell:buy (S/B) ratio, which is the number of insider sell decisions divided by the number of insider buy decisions. This ratio, originated by me in 1971, will enable us to ascertain what the insiders collectively are thinking at any time.

Many analysts (but not enough) follow this S/B ratio. Among them are Martin Zweig; Bob Nurock (Wall $treet Week); the Professional Tapereader (Stan Weinstein); William Scheinman; numerous fund managers, such as Fidelity, Putnam, and T.

Rowe Price; and stock brokerage houses such as E. F. Hutton, Merrill Lynch, and Prudential Bache.

Over the course of years it has become apparent that insiders sell at least twice as much of their own company's stock as they buy. There are many reasons for an insider to sell: diversification, college educations, second house, perhaps a divorce settlement. Keep in mind, however, that if the insider thought his stock would materially increase in value, he could raise money by other means. For instance, he could put the stock up as loan collateral instead of selling it. There is only *one* reason for him to buy on the open market (i.e., pay the same price that you or I would have to pay): He believes that the value of his company's stock will increase. When an insider buys on the open market, he does so for only *one* reason: He believes his company to be the best investment available. It is human to see the problems, mistakes, and inefficiences of the firm we work for. Sometimes we wonder how it even survives. We forget its good attributes. So, when an insider buys stock in his own company, it can only be construed as a highly optimistic action.

The Effect of Option Plans on the S/B

When this book was almost completed, I changed the normal sell:buy ratio from 2 to 2.5 because of the great increase in corporate option plans. As the market broke loose in 1982, options became profitable and wanted. In the flat market of the 1960s and 1970s, options were somewhat discarded because they failed to "get in the money" and offered little incentive to executives. With the better market, options became valuable and option plans proliferated. Long stock is sometimes sold to pay for cheap option stock, and because options are a form of compensation (but have to be sold to become compensation), this translates into insider selling. Thus the increase of the "normal" S/B to 2.5.

It is an extremely bullish situation when corporate officers exercise options *and* simultaenously buy on the open market. This was the case with Allied–Signal's spin-off of the Henley

Group in April 1986. Henley insiders were given tremendous amounts of options to leave Allied, and 15 Henley officers bought 191,660 shares on the open market at the time of the spin-off. Henley sold at $17 soon after the spin-off. The issue recently sold at $30.

As already mentioned in Chapter 2, any options that are exercised or awarded are reported on Form 4.

The S/B Formula

An S/B of 2.5 means that for every buy there are 2.5 sales by insiders. The S/B for a particular week is obtained by dividing all insider sales by all insider buys.

$$S \div B = S/B$$

The S/B is composed of only listed stocks because they are less volatile and have a more seasoned market. Thus, if in one week there are 100 sales transactions by insiders and 40 buys, this would be normal activity:

$$100 \div 40 = 2.5$$

Notice that the ratio takes no account of dollar amount, price, or any characteristic other than B (buy) or S (sale). Every open market trade by an insider is an investment decision, and this is what we are after—*each* insider's thoughts.

Direct and Indirect Holdings by Insiders

Stock can change hands by means other than through open-market trades. Insiders often dispose of stock through gifts— either to family or to charities. Such a gift is usually made for tax reasons and cannot be construed as an investment decision. And stock can be acquired by the exercise of options, through company profit sharing plans, or by dividends or stock splits. None of these is an open-market transaction or an investment decision. They should not be considered in our analysis. Fortunately, the insider has to identify the nature of his acquisition or disposal on Form 4. Thus, we can easily identify and exclude changes that are not open-market transactions.

In addition to direct beneficial holdings, the insider has to report trades in which he has an indirect interest. Family-owned and 100%-owned vehicles or trusts can be reported as being indirect, but for our purposes they are the same as direct. Even when he might not have beneficial ownership, the insider with an indirect interest has some degree of control over the stock. It is best to combine the direct and indirect transactions and holdings that an insider has reported on Form 4. Then we can see the complete picture, not only of his transactions but also of his complete holdings. Then we are able to arrive at a correct percentage of his stock that he has traded.

Although some indirect holdings are only remotely controlled by the insider, many are his vehicle only. For our purposes, any such holdings should be combined with his claimed direct holdings. Because indirect holdings can be a preponderant percentage of an insider's reported holdings and because we cannot ascertain his degree of control, we combine all indirect with direct holdings.

Insider Trades and Past Market Performance

Since 1971, I have plotted the S/B ratio because I believe that insiders as a group can give us outsiders a clue as to the course of the economy (i.e., the market). Each week I count the number of insider sell transactions and divide by the number of buy transactions. If in one week there are 200 sales and 100 buys, then the ratio is 2:1—twice as many sales as buys. The higher the ratio, the more sales are being transacted and the more bearish are the insiders. Perhaps it would be clearer if the buys were divided by the sales—then higher numbers would indicate more insider buying. However, my partner refused to have a B/S ratio! So, S/B it is. And that is why the S/B ratio is inverted in the graphs shown in Figures 4–1 through 4–4 (see pages 28–31). The graphs validate the hypothesis that the intensity of insider buying and selling can call the market.

Figure 4–1 shows that there was rapid improvement from 1971 in the S/B ratio even with the market falling from above 900 to 800. The insiders then sold when the market recovered to 950, but they quickly reversed and correctly foretold the 1975 bull market in which the Dow appreciated 70%. The S/B ratio flirted below a very bullish 1.0 for most of 1974.

It is important to comment on 1974. The insiders were "wrong" in their buying throughout the year; the market during that period fell almost a third. As can be imagined, such a prolonged drop led to almost total lack of confidence in investors' minds, especially because in the previous year there had been a drop of more than 200 points.

I have mentioned previously that insiders should give us confidence so that we can be patient—or, at least, objective. Although the wait was prolonged, insiders were right, as usual, and the market amply rewarded patience. The next year, 1975, smartly appreciated (70%), as the insiders had predicted it would.

From 1976 through 1978, the S/B gyrated from a low of 4.0 with the market at a high of 1029 to 2.5 with the market near its low at 735. Insiders were not overly impressed with a market that penetrated 1000 four times in 1976 and that during the last quarter of that year foretold a subsequent 1977 drop of 250 points (25%).

The insiders aptly predicted the nine-month market rise in 1978.

Market tops in August 1979, January 1980, and March through May 1981 could be identified by insider trading. Lows in November 1979, March 1980, and September 1981 also were foretold.

However, the overall view, with repeated bullish readings from 1979 to 1983 (with the S/B repeatedly at or near 1.0), was telling the astute observer of the emergence of the Great Bull Market that commenced with a bang in August 1982 and is still in place today.

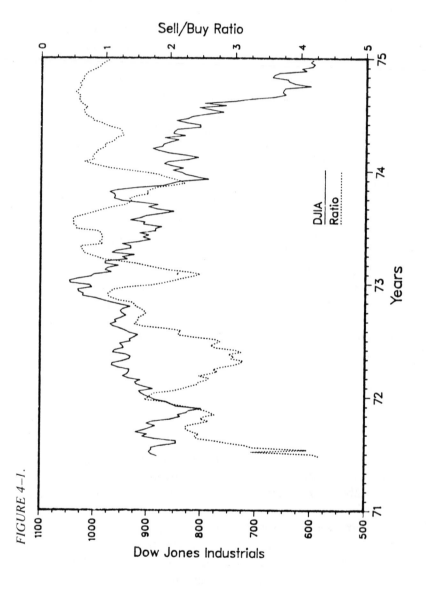

FIGURE 4-1.

28

FIGURE 4-2.

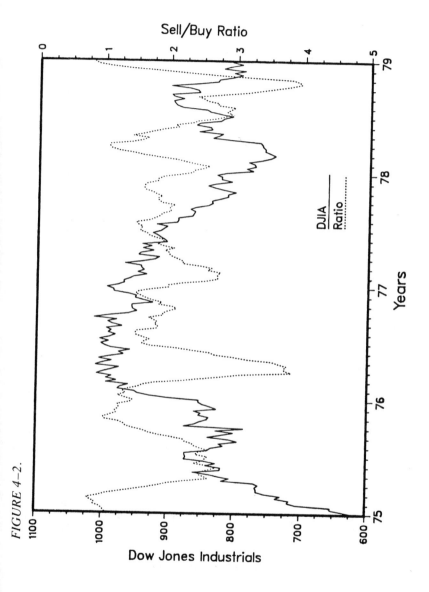

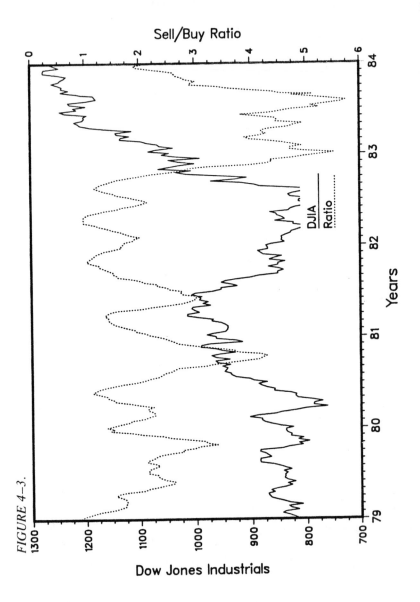

FIGURE 4–3.

30

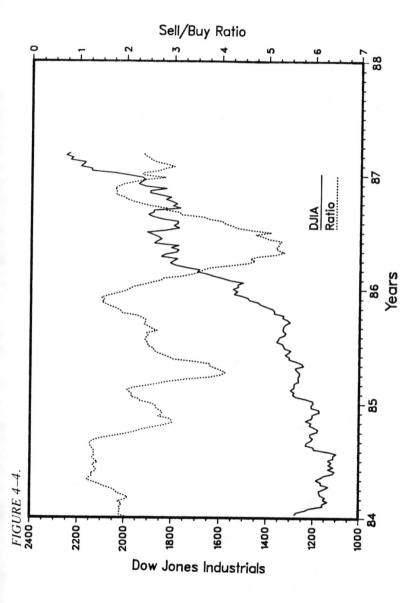

FIGURE 4-4.

In 1981 to 1982 the insiders four times equaled their open-market sell trades with buy orders. This was a first in my experience, especially because the buying ran parallel with a major market retreat that lasted 14 months and shaved 25% off market value by April 1981.

In practically all of 1984 there were bullish S/B ratios, whereas the market ended the year close to where it started. From a 4.0 reading in May 1985, the S/B ratio rallied and four months later so did the market—all the way from 1225 to 1800 in early 1986.

The market hit new highs of over 1800 in March 1986, but then for the rest of the year it bumped around at plus or minus 1800. In May, however, the insiders became extremely bullish, and we saw another first: At a market high point, the insiders' S/B ratio improved in a straight line from 5.3 to nearly 1.0 (where buying equals selling). A look at Figure 4–4 shows how clairvoyant the insiders were in calling the 1987 market explosion. The market in January 1987 shook off its lethargy and in three months moved from 1900 to 2400. In August, it exceeded 2700.

Table 4–1 shows what happened the last 17 times that the S/B ratio dropped below 2.0 from higher levels. Sixteen successes out of 18 occurrences is not bad forecasting at all.

It is interesting to gauge the average point increase in the Dow after each penetration and the time that elapsed to the subsequent high. The 16 occurrences went up an average 190 points in an average of 6.4 months for an average gain of 19% ($19 \times 16 = 304\%$, or an annualized gain of 36%). Astounding!

An unusual happening is when insiders *buy* more stock than they *sell*. The insiders heralded the Big Bull Market that started in August 1982, as evidenced by the fact that the S/B was below 1.0 (net buying) in late 1981. This happened twice more in 1982. The weekly readings in mid-1984 showed more insider buying than selling, and the market enjoyed its subsequent 1100-point leg-up in 1985–1986.

The unique occurrence referred to on page 18 is shown graphically in Figure 4–4. You can see there that the insiders abruptly increased their buying while the market was floundering

TABLE 4–1.

S/B Goes Below 2.0	DJIA	Subsequent DJIA High	DOW
December 1971	860	April 1972	960
July 1972	940	February 1973	1,040
January 1973	Insiders Bought Early		
November 1973	780	March 1974	880
September 1975	835	March 1976	1,000
May 1976	960	October 1976	1,020
November 1976	950	January 1977	990
June 1977	Insiders Bought Early		
February 1978	740	August 1978	900
November 1978	780	April 1979	875
October 1979	810	February 1980	900
March 1980	775	November 1981	975
January 1981	940	March 1981	1,010
June 1982	780	November 1983	1,275
March 1984	1,150	July 1984	1,350
October 1985	1,350	June 1986	1,915
November 1986	2,000	April 1986	2,400
May 13, 1987	2,330	August 1987	2,740

around at an all-time high reading. Insiders do not buy at market highs—generally.

This leads to a hypothesis. If a time ever arrives when the market is making pronounced lows concurrent with heavy insider selling, then the doomsayers of the time will probably be correct! It is to be hoped that we will never see this occurrence, but beware if we do! Fortunately, it has not occurred in recent history.

Figures 4–1 to 4–4 illustrate one truism. The insiders, although near-perfect in their ability to tell us when to buy, sometimes sell too early. It is almost axiomatic that they cash in prematurely in bull markets. Examples are early 1975, early 1976, and, most pronounced, the first seven months of 1983.

Protecting Capital and Profits

Individual stocks perform independently of the general market, especially in a period of a steady stock market. As mentioned earlier, however, the market's most pronounced moves take place in relatively short spurts or retreats. During periods of market advances, most stocks appreciate, and in declines most stocks go south in unison. Also, it is characteristic that in bear markets stocks retreat faster than they appreciate in bull markets. Thus, although preservation of capital should be paramount, it seems to be a difficult task for most investors.

Gerald M. Loeb's classic *Battle for Investment Survival* (Hurry House Publishers, N.Y., 1952) put forth the all-important investment commandment: "Cut your losses and let your profit run: sell when your stock depreciates 10%." If we employ that advice and improve on it, then we don't care if the insiders do not. By entering the market with the insiders—usually when only doom is being spouted by the prophets—we then sit and let our profits run. It is expedient to place stop-loss sell orders (Loeb's 10%?) as the market climbs, however. A stock that depreciates 10%, especially in a strong market, merits profit-taking.

We buy when the S/B ratio reaches 1.5. This is *mandatory*. We can see that our 16-year graphs in Figures 4–1 to 4–4 almost never fail to register a bull market soon after S/B 1.5 is reached. Subsequent sales, however, are subject to a more complicated formula.

The Stop-Loss Order

Sales are not effected if the S/B ratio catapults above the S/B 2.0 level. So how are capital and profits protected? There is a mechanism that can be employed: the stop-loss order.

A stop-loss order is a price that you give to your broker that is below the market. If that price is reached, either on the "floor" or in the NASDAQ (OTC market) system, then your stop-loss order becomes a market order. The next sale is yours at the next bid.

By employing the stop-loss order, you let your profits run as the market continues to gain, but when it falters, your stop-loss order protects you from a sizable loss. Besides letting your profits run and cutting short your losses, the stop-loss gives you the discipline to sell. Most investors buy easily—but sell hard. They become wedded to a stock or an idea, and they hope that time will bail them out. "It'll come back," they say. Most times it won't.

After our entry into the market when the S/B touches 1.5, we do not necessarily employ the stop-loss technique until the S/B passes the 2.0 level. The odds are immensely in our favor that the market will rise—and we have entered the market near the low. It may have a few more points to retreat, though, and we do not want to be "stopped out" here. Most often, though, when the S/B has risen from 1.5 to 2.0, the market has usually been rising too. These assumptions can be illustrated (i.e., proven) by consulting Figures 4–1 through 4–4.

At this point, we initiate our stop-loss plan. It is a two-tier technique. To ride the market (don't fight the tape), we place in our *minds* a stop-loss on the *market*. That is, we will *not* place stops on our individual stocks until the market retreats 5%. A 5% stop-loss on a stock is very tight. Most stocks can go down that much in a single day. But 5% on the entire market (i.e., the Dow Jones industrials) is a substantial and *serious* drop and should result in further market correction or a genuine bear market.

Suppose that the Dow is at 1900 and we are totally invested because the S/B is at 1.5. But the S/B weakens and hits 2.5, so we put our mental stop-loss at 5% below any subsequent market high. The Dow reaches 1960 and then falls 99 points to 1861 (5%): At this point, we give definite stop-loss orders to our broker on each of our stocks. But at what prices? Many market analysts suggest 10%, but we are fairly certain of lower markets, so I suggest tightening to around 6 to 7%.

The Beta

One refinement that can be successfully employed to determine the price at which to place a stop-loss order is tailoring the stop-loss by using a stock's beta. The beta measures a stock's volatility vis-à-vis the market. A stock with a beta of 1 should act the same as the market—that is, appreciate or depreciate the same percentage as the market. Higher or lower numbers should see corresponding movement. Thus, a stock with a beta of 1.5 should move 50% more in either direction than the general market does. A beta of 0.9 should move 10% less than the market moves.

Use betas to price a stop-loss order. Thus, put a stop-loss order on a stock with a 1.5 beta priced 12% below the stock's current price. A stock with a beta of 0.5 warrants a stop-loss at 5% below its current price. Several services, such as *Value Line* and Martin Zweig's *Security Screen,* supply betas. I prefer to chart a stock with the Dow to arrive at my own feeling for a stock's volatility, and then to assign my own beta.

Preventing Whipsawing

The two-tier stop-loss system helps to prevent being whipsawed out of the market prematurely. If the market retreats 5%, then each of our stocks will have to retreat from the price at which they then are selling. Probably we have lost some points during the market's 5% retreat, and we will lose more if our stops are executed. But I think the protection from being whipsawed is worth the exposure to a bit more potential loss.

Loeb's 10% seems to be a drastic formula, especially in today's markets, because a 10% move in some stocks can happen easily. A stock with a high beta would easily be sold too early. The market can be temporarily as wrong as all get-out. If we don't have the confidence, patience, and prescience of the insiders, we will be whipsawed unmercifully.

As the market kicks off our stop-loss orders, if it does, we put the proceeds in cash equivalents (e.g., money market funds). Reinvestment is not effected until the S/B ratio again falls to 1.5. Eventually it will. Patience is required.

5

The Five-Step Insiders'
Timing Formula

The Five-Step Insiders' Timing Formula is of utmost importance. A graphic presentation (see Figure 5–1 on page 40) that sums up all the discussion in the previous chapters should help you to fully understand its precepts. A caveat: You still are subject to the uncertainties of your individual investments. The Insiders' Timing Formula is a great aid and comfort, but it does not preclude constant vigilance over your stock selections. Investment decisions can't be cast in cement. For example, a 10% slash in price for a particular stock may dictate preventive precedence over the Insiders' Timing Formula.

Tables 5–1 to 5–3 (see pages 43–48 and 50–53) prove the validity of the Insiders' Timing Formula.

FIGURE 5-1. *Five-Step Insiders' Timing Formula—Hypothetical Illustration.*

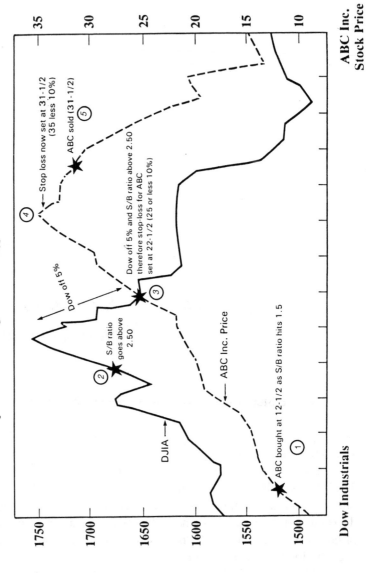

Dow Industrials

ABC Inc.
Stock Price

Step One—Stock Bought

In our hypothetical example shown in Figure 5–1, the stock of ABC Inc. is bought when the S/B ratio reaches 1.5. In the figure, the dashed line represents the price of the stock, and the solid line represents the Dow Jones Industrial Average.

Step Two—Insiders Flash Caution Signal

When the S/B ratio goes above 2.5, corporate managers are warning us that either the market has outrun intrinsic value or the economy will probably weaken. We put a mental stop-loss on the market so that a 5% retreat from any subsequent high forces us to employ stop-losses to all of our stocks.

Step Three—Dow Then Retreats

At the point at which the DJIA is off 5% and the S/B ratio is above 2.5, the investor places a stop-loss order for ABC Inc. at $22.50 ($25, or less 10%).

Step Four—Stop-Loss Placed On Our Stocks

Step Five—Stock Sold

The stock has continued to rise to this point, but finally succumbs and joins the general market retreat. Therefore, at this point the stock falls, our adjusted stop-loss order of $31.50 has been reached, and the ABC Inc. stock is sold.

Table 5–1 shows the results of buying and selling the Dow as a package and records the Dow points made and (lost) during this period.

Purchasing began in January 1976 when the S/B was below 1.5. The Dow managed by the Insiders' Formula racked up 1077 points during the 10-years whereas the Dow itself gained only 892 points. The Dow managed by the Insiders' Formula gained 21% over the actual Dow. An additional and substantial profit was realized because we were out of the market (40% of the time) and earning high money market interest.

The stocks in Table 5–2 (see pages 46–48) were chosen to illustrate the efficacy of the formula. These six stocks, having a common denominator in their name, were bought and sold on the same dates as the Dow in Table 5–1. (Remember, the studies in this book are strictly objective and under no circumstance pick and choose to make a point.) This arbitrarily chosen group encompasses six different industries, which is about as objective as you can get.

This arbitrary selection of six blue-chip stocks that begin with the name "General" outperformed the DJIA by a 36.88% margin, and kept us out of the market 40% of the time. The total interest earned on our holdings during the period when we were out of the market amounted to an additional return of nearly 41%.

Yet we have not put the Insiders' Timing Formula into full gear. Stop-loss orders were not placed on the individual stocks after the S/B and a 5% market retreat signaled an upcoming bear market.

Each time the six stocks are sold by the Timing Formula, the net profit (or loss) is recorded. The end result of the Insiders' Timing Formula is that it achieved a 230% profit. Think what the appreciation could have been had we not been confined to the six "Generals" for the entire 10 years!

Table 5–3 (see pages 50–53) uses the same dates as the previous two tables. We always buy at S/B 1.5. But at S/B 2.0 we place stop-loss orders on the market 5% below any subsequent high it might attain. In this study, a 5% retreat from each stock's subsequent high price triggers execution of our stop-loss orders. Ordinarily, we would be more artful in setting the stop-loss prices, as commented on previously, by using betas.

TABLE 5-1. Trading the DJIA by Formula.

Action B—Buy S—Sell	Date	S/B	DJIA	(Depreciation) Appreciation in Points
B	1/5/76	1.35	865	
	Subsequent high 1014 stop loss at 963 (1014-5%)			
S	10/15/76	2.57	963	98
B	12/8/76	1.50	963	
	Subsequent high 955 stop loss at 945 (995-5%)			
S	2/15/77	2.74	945	(15)
B	7/25/77	1.49	888	
	Stop loss at 843 (888-5%)			
S	9/19/77	2.08	843	(45)
B	3/6/78	1.43	751	
	Stop loss at 820			
S	7/3/78	2.83	820	69

TABLE 5-1. (continued)

Action B—Buy S—Sell	Date	S/B	DJIA	(Depreciation) Appreciation in Points
B	12/4/78	1.40	822	
S	Stop loss at 842 10/15/79	3.09	842	20
B	12/17/79	1.46	839	
S	Stop loss at 859 2/12/80	2.26	859	20
B	4/28/80	1.41	817	
S	Stop loss at 941 12/23/80	2.62	941	124
B	2/23/81	1.49	954	
S	Stop loss at 964 7/15/81	2.53	964	10

TABLE 5-1. (continued)

Action B—Buy S—Sell	Date	S/B	DJIA	(Depreciation) Appreciation in Points
B	9/21/81	1.42	841	
S	Stop loss at 844 1/29/82	2.00	844	3
B	3/8/82	1.26	805	
S	Stop loss at 821 6/22/82	2.04	797	(8)
B	8/2/82	1.36	803	
S	Stop loss at 1012 10/20/82	2.82	1012	209
B	4/15/84	1.48	1165	
S	Stop loss at 1757 5/21/86	6.33	1757	592
B	10/15/86	1.18	1831	
	Present stop loss at 2574 (2710–5%)			

TABLE 5–2. The Performance of the "Generals."

	Buy 1/5/76	Sell 10/15/76	Buy 12/8/76	Sell 2/15/77	Buy 7/25/77	Sell 9/19/77
General Dynamics	9	10	12	13	13	12
General Electric	24	26	26	26	28	27
General Instrument	3	5	6	7	7	7
General Mills	30	32	34	30	31	29
General Motors	66	70	73	71	69	66
General Telephone	26	29	30	29	33	31
		+8.86%		−2.76%		−11.05%

	Buy 3/6/78	Sell 7/3/78	Buy 12/4/78	Sell 10/5/79	Buy 12/17/79	Sell 2/12/80
General Dynamics	9	11	18	24	30	39
General Electric	23	25	24	26	25	28
General Instrument	7	10	10	15	16	17
General Mills	28	30	23	27	27	34
General Motors	58	59	55	65	52	53
General Telephone	29	29	27	28	28	28
		+6.49%		+17.83%		+11.80%

TABLE 5-2. (continued)

	Buy 4/28/80	Sell 12/23/80	Buy 2/23/81	Sell 7/15/81	Buy 9/21/81	Sell 1/29/82
General Dynamics	35	37	30	39	24	26
General Electric	24	31	34	32	27	32
General Instrument	15	29	26	35	34	41
General Mills	23	27	27	34	35	34
General Motors	45	47	48	49	45	38
General Telephone	27	28	25	29	30	31
		+17.75%		+14.74%		+3.60%

	Buy 3/8/82	Sell 6/22/82	Buy 8/2/82	Sell 10/20/82	Buy 4/16/84	Sell 5/21/86
General Dynamics	19	29	29	36	48	76
General Electric	30	31	39	43	55	77
General Instrument	32	34	37	50	25	22
General Mills	37	42	44	53	48	75
General Motors	39	47	44	55	65	75
General Telephone	29	27	28	40	39	51
		+12.90%		+25.33%		+34.29%

TABLE 5–2. (continued)

	Buy 10/15/86	Sell 3/20/87
General Dynamics	72	76
General Electric	73	107
General Instrument	19	28
General Mills	33x	53
General Motors	67	78
General Telephone	34x	42

The recap of the 10 years covered by Tables 5–3 is as follows:

- The Dow appreciated 105% if bought and held the entire period.

- The Dow increased this gain about 20% if one bought the average at S/B 1.5 and sold at 2.0.

- The "Generals" portfolio appreciated 140% when, as a package, the stocks were bought at S/B 1.5 and sold at S/B 2.0.

- The complete Insiders' Timing Formula (using a mental market stop and then applying actual stops to the different stocks) showed a 242% profit.

- By being out of the market for a substantial time when the market was doing nothing or retreating, our profits grew another 40% from interest earned in money market accounts.

The formula-managed "Generals" portfolio appreciated 242%, whereas the Dow came in with a 105% profit. Remember that most money managers, funds, and so on are mightily pleased to consistently match the Dow. Again, for a good percentage of time we were in cash and earning high interest, plus our exposure (i.e., risk) was reduced.

We can summarize our results from January 1976 to July 1986 as follows:

- The DJIA appreciated 105%.

- The DJIA managed by the Insiders' Market Formula appreciated 126%.

- The "Generals" portfolio managed by the Insiders' Market Formula appreciated 140%.

- The "Generals" portfolio managed by the stop-loss Insiders' Timing Formula appreciated 242%.

Each stock appreciated, whether held for the 10 years or managed by using the formula. The results were as shown in

TABLE 5–3. The "Generals" Performance with a Stop-Loss at 5%.

	Buy	Sell	Buy	Sell	Buy	Sell
General Dynamics	Jan. 76 9	Nov. 76 10	Dec. 76 12	Mar. 77 13	July 77 13	Sept. 77 12
General Electric	24	Oct. 76 25	Dec. 76 26	Aug. 77 27	Mar. 78 23	Sept. 78 27
General Instrument	3	Nov. 76 7	Dec. 76 6	Mar. 77 7	July 77 7	Sept. 77 6
General Mills	30	Feb. 77 33	July 77 31	Sept. 77 28	Mar. 78 28	Sept. 78 33
General Motors	66	Feb. 77 76	July 77 69	Nov. 77 63	Mar. 78 58	July 78 56
General Telephone	26	Feb. 77 31	July 77 33	Sept. 77 30	Mar. 78 29	Oct. 78 31
		+15.2%		−5.1%		+4.4%

TABLE 5–3. (continued)

	Buy	Sell	Buy	Sell	Buy	Sell
General Dynamics	Mar. 78	Oct. 78	Dec. 78	Jan. 80	Apr. 80	Jan. 81
	9	17	18	40	35	42
General Electric	Dec. 78	Oct. 79	Dec. 79	Feb. 80	Apr. 80	May 80
	24	25	25	27	24	33
General Instrument	Mar. 78	Oct. 78	Dec. 78	Mar. 80	Apr. 80	Dec. 80
	7	13	10	17	15	28
General Mills	Dec. 78	Oct. 79	Dec. 79	Feb. 80	Apr. 80	July 81
	23	26	27	24	23	38
General Motors	Dec. 78	Nov. 79	Dec. 79	Mar. 80	Apr. 80	July 81
	55	62	52	50	45	56
General Telephone	Dec. 78	Jan. 80	Apr. 80	Dec. 80	Feb. 81	Jan. 82
	27	28	27	27	25	31
		+17.9%		+16.4%		+36.5%

TABLE 5–3. (continued)

	Buy	Sell	Buy	Sell	Buy	Sell
General Dynamics	Feb. 81 / 30	July 81 / 37	Sept. 81 / 24	Feb. 82 / 26	Mar. 82 / 19	Oct. 82 / 35
General Electric	Feb. 81 / 34	July 81 / 31	Sept. 81 / 27	Apr. 82 / 32	Mar. 82 / 30	July 83 / 55
General Instrument	Feb. 81 / 26	July 81 / 33	Sept. 81 / 34	Jan. 82 / 39	Mar. 82 / 32	July 82 / 38
General Mills	Sept. 81 / 35	July 81 / 53	Sept. 81	Not bought again until		
General Motors	Sept. 81 / 45	Feb. 82 / 36	Mar. 82 / 39	Feb. 84 / 76	Not bought again until	
General Telephone	Mar. 82 / 29	July 83 / 45	Not bought again until			
		+18.1%		+39.5%		+58%

TABLE 5–3. (continued)

					Buy
General Dynamics	Not bought again until		Apr. 84 48	July 86 77	Oct. 86 72
General Electric	Not bought again until		Apr. 84 55	July 86 79	Oct. 86 73
General Instrument	. . . . Aug. 82 37	Feb. 28 57	Apr. 84 25	June 86 24	Oct. 86 19
General Mills	. . . .		Apr. 84 48	July 86 85	Oct. 86 66
General Motors	. . . .		Apr. 84 65	June 86 84	Oct. 86 67
General Telephone	. . . .		Apr. 84 39	July 86 54	Oct. 86 45
				+43.9%	

Table 5–4. Astounding—yes, complicated—no, reasonable—yes. We have merely engaged for our own a research department that consists of thousands of America's corporate managers.

TABLE 5–4. Appreciation in the "Generals" Stock.

	Held for 10 Years	*Managed by Formula*
General Dynamics	63	105
General Electric	52	69
General Instrument	16	67
General Mills	56	75
General Motors	4	65
General Telephone	33	42
	224*	423*

*The total of column 1 is 53% of the total of column 2.

The insiders are very, very good at calling the fortunes of their respective companies and even better at collectively calling the market trend. However, we know that they are early sellers, and sometimes they just cannot anticipate surprise developments. We have to protect ourselves from a scenario in which for some reason the insiders err. At least we can preserve capital or increase profits by going with the market and against the insiders.

The important adage of "not fighting the tape" leads to an additional protective device: When either long or short, place a drastic 10% stop-loss on the market. If long, and the Dow retreats 10%, sell. If short, and the market goes up 10%, cover. But again, do this by using stop-loss orders; it still might be possible to ride out the storm and return to our Insiders' Formula.

Changed conditions and study of insiders' actions would certainly dictate a change of holdings and would increase profitable results from using the Insiders' Formula. This is impossible to reconstruct, because each individual would select different stocks, but the results of a study of high beta stocks that were traded over the 10 years are shown in Table 5–5 (see pages 56–58).

The managed portfolio shown in Table 5–5, consisting of IBM, MMM, Philip Morris, Delta Air, Pfizer, Integrated Resources, CBS, and Dupont would have appreciated 261% by using the Insiders' Timing Formula. By buying and holding for the 10 years, a 174% profit would have been achieved. The formula outperformed the buy and hold method by 50%.

The Insiders' Timing Formula as presented so far has had us enter the market only at S/B 1.5. To enter at this point is *mandatory*. However, a refinement should be interjected here.

Refer back to Table 4–1 (on page 33). It appears that when the market goes below S/B 2.0, a substantial rise can be anticipated. Therefore, it seems prudent not to wait for S/B 1.5. The odds are vastly in our favor that if an S/B substantially above 2.0 falls below 2.0, we can garner more profits in more time than waiting for S/B 1.5.

If the insiders then resume selling, we can quickly leave the market by using our standard sell formula:

1. The S/B is over 2.5.

2. The market retreats by 5%.

3. The stock(s) we hold are stopped.

A goodly amount of time, though, the market will be in a descendency straight through the S/B, and we have no excuse for entering it at an earlier level.

If this book does nothing else, it is my hope that it contributes to the demise of the "investment" practice of buying and burying stocks. The hope that a company is so-o-o-o good that its stock can be bought and tenaciously held on to 'til death do us part is ridiculous.

The previous studies showed that we can harness market fluctuations to maximize profit. That alone should be enough to do away with the hold-forever theory. How can anyone be so presumptuous as to pronounce that a company—much less an industry—will remain dominant ad infinitum!

TABLE 5–5. *A Study of High Beta Stocks.*

	Beta	Buy	Sell	Buy	Sell	Buy	Sell	Buy	Sell
IBM	1.05	Jan. 76 60	Oct. 79 67	Dec. 79 65	Feb. 80 60	Apr. 80 52	May 86 151		
MMM	1.05	Jan. 76 57	Oct. 78 65	Dec. 78 62	Oct. 79 50	Dec. 79 48	Dec. 80 62		
		Feb. 81 60	July 81 57	Sept. 81 49	Aug. 83 84	Apr. 84 74	Aug. 86 108		
CBS	1.10	Jan. 76 48	Oct. 76 59	Dec. 76 57	Sept. 79 56	Mar. 78 46	July 78 61		
		Dec. 78 52	Oct. 79 55	Dec. 79 49	Feb. 80 46	Apr. 80 44	July 81 60		
		Sept. 81 52	Jan. 82 48	Mar. 82 40	June 82 38	Aug. 82 45	Oct. 82 80		
		Apr. 84 77	Aug. 86 143						

TABLE 5–5. (continued)

	Beta	Buy	Sell	Buy	Sell	Buy	Sell
Pfizer	1.05	Jan. 76 13	Oct. 76 14	Dec. 76 14	Apr. 74 13	July 77 13	Sept. 78 19
		Dec. 78 17	Mar. 80 19	Apr. 80 20	July 81 25	Sept. 81 21	July 82 28
		Aug. 82	Oct. 83 38	Apr. 84 35	July 86 68		
Dupont	1.15	Jan. 76 43	May 77 41	July 77 40	Feb. 78 38	Mar. 78 35	Sept. 78 48
		Dec. 78 42	Oct. 79 44	Dec. 79 41	Mar. 80 39	Apr. 80 38	Dec. 80 43
		Feb. 81 49	July 81 48	Sept. 81 40	June 82 32	Aug. 82 32	Oct. 82 44
		Apr. 84 50	Sept. 86 84				

TABLE 5–5. (continued)

	Beta	Buy	Sell	Buy	Sell	Buy	Sell
Delta Air	1.10	Jan. 76 19	Jan. 77 19	Feb. 77 17	Sept. 78 27	Dec. 78 21	Feb. 80 20
		Apr. 80 17	July 81 39	Sept. 81 28	Jan. 82 26	Mar. 82 30	July 82 36
		Aug. 82 27	Oct. 82 37	Apr. 84 37	May 86 47		
Philip Morris	1.00	Jan. 76 14	Oct. 76 16	Dec. 76 16	Feb. 77 14	July 77 15	Nov. 77 15
		Mar. 78 15	Sept. 78 18	Dec. 78 18	Oct. 79 17	Dec. 79 16	May 81 29
		Sept. 81 24	Aug. 86 74				
Integrated Resources	1.35	Mar. 78 3	Feb. 80 11	Apr. 80 7	Dec. 80 14	Feb. 81 11	July 81 12
		Sept. 81 9	June 83 41	Apr. 84 24	May 86 28		

58

The following stocks, even after the biggest bull market ever experienced, sold in 1986 below their highs of *many* years ago. They all were previously considered to be such blue chips that they were candidates to be bought and buried:

Texas Instruments	Burroughs Corp (Unisys)
Western Union	U.S. Steel (USX Corp)
Union Pacific	Avon Products
Timken	Bank America
Schering-Plough	Union Carbide
Reynolds Metals	Mobil Oil
Prime Computer	General Motors
W.R. Grace	Xerox
Eastern Airlines	International Harvester (Navistar)
Caterpillar Tractor	Black & Decker
Bethlehem Steel	Eastman Kodak
Standard Oil of California	Polaroid
(Chevron)	
Great Atlantic & Pacific Tea	
—and many more.	

Giant U.S. Steel in 1941 sold at 70. No one at the time could have contemplated that 45 years later the stock would be mired at a third that price. The retailing darling of the early part of the century—F.W. Woolworth—proved to be a fizzler for the next 80 years. Ultra-safe utilities (formerly known as "widow stocks") were expected to have a 10% yearly growth. Instead, they were upended by double-digit inflation, and interest rates and the expenses of nuclear plant disasters. General Motors, the world's biggest manufacturer, sold for $80 per share in 1972. Fourteen years later it sold at 66.

6

Profiting in a Bear Market

The basic trend of the market determines our participation in it. When the market *and* the insiders are bullish, we are full participants. We do not fight the tape or go contrary. No thought of selling short is entertained unless we are in a falling market with insiders selling.

We can really look forward to a bear market because the Insiders' Timing Formula will separate us from most other managers. We are planning to go as much as 100% short (selling what we do not have and hopefully replacing it at lower prices). In a bear market, a larger percentage of all stocks retreat than go up in a bull market. Also, stock prices are pared in bear markets a lot faster and more harshly than they go up in bull markets.

Studies of stocks with low insider ratings (see Table 8-8 on pages 107–109) have shown that in bull markets the preponderance of these stocks appreciate materially less than does the general market. Ipso facto, in a bear market we can expect them to depreciate more than does the general market.

The Big Bull Market has lasted so long that we have to go back to 1981 to find the last bear market, which commenced in January and lasted until the current bull rampaged. The stocks in Table 6–1 (on pages 63–67) were multiple sales in 1981—that is, five net sales constituted a multiple sale by insiders.

Insiders—that is, portfolios chosen to consist of stocks with high insider ratings—consistently out-gain the Dow. Portfolios consisting of stocks with low insider ratings should then underperform the Dow. If this is the case, then we can feel as comfortable with short positions in a bear market as we would with high-rated insider stocks in a rising market.

Stocks listed in Table 6–1 that were rated low by the insiders were off almost 50% more than the DJIA; 49 stocks (68%) underperformed the Dow.

Study by industry group of the stocks in Table 6–1 is interesting; it shows how they react in a bear market. Foods, long described as defensive stocks, did very well—Great A&P, Sysco, Pepsico, McDonald's. Mass retailers did well—J.C. Penney, Wal-Mart, and Sears. Drugs were all right—Abbott Labs, Matrix, Syntex, and Smithkline. Industrials—forget 'em: Harnischfeger, Owens Corning, Revere Copper & Brass, Gulton. All high-tech stocks suffered because investors became wary of the high P/E ratios of those stocks in a bear market.

Reading and Bates, Dresser, Ashland, and Schlumberger were sliced 50% in value from their listing in 1981 until July 30, 1982. Had an investor been able to ascertain that oil stocks had five diastrous years ahead, and had that investor gone short on these four oil stocks, he could have made a fortune.

The extensive list in Table 6-1 is presented to show that the performance of 72 stocks, which by its length should have

TABLE 6–1. Stocks with Multiple Sales by Insiders.

Date Stock Recorded, Five Net Insider Sales	Stock	1981 Price	July 30, 1982 Price	Percentage Gain or Loss
January 7	Archer Daniels Midland	24	13	(46)
	Matrix	20	20	—
January 14	Barnes Engineering	9	3	(67)
	International Controls	24	13	(46)
	Owens Corning Fiberglas	27	17	(37)
	Sears Roebuck	16	19	19
	Smithkline	76	63	(17)
	Whittaker Corp.	29	20	(31)
January 21	Revere Copper & Brass	17	9	(47)
	Tektronix	56	45	(20)
	Englehard	47	21	(55)
	Great Western Financial	17	12	(29)
	Masco	29	31	7
	Merrill Lynch	34	25	(27)
	J.C. Penney	23	39	70
	Prime Computer	34	18	(47)
	Publicker Industries	7	2	(71)
	Reading & Bates	32	11	(66)

TABLE 6–1. (continued)

Date Stock Recorded, Five Net Insider Sales	Stock	1981 Price	July 30, 1982 Price	Percentage Gain or Loss
January 28	Comdisco	20	18	(10)
	Dresser Industries	48	15	(69)
	General Motors	44	43	(2)
	Hilton Hotels	37	32	(14)
	E.F. Hutton	29	27	(2)
	National Can	21	17	(19)
	RLC Corp.	14	10	(29)
	Raytheon	48	39	(19)
	Syntex Corp.	30	38	27
	U.S. Home	28	13	(54)
February 4	American Medical Intl.	30	24	(20)
	American Motor Inns	14	17	21
	E Systems	41	34	(17)
	Health-Chem	21	6	(71)

TABLE 6-1. (continued)

Date Stock Recorded, Five Net Insider Sales	Stock	1981 Price	July 30, 1982 Price	Percentage Gain or Loss
February 11	Abbott Labs	29	30	3
	American Broadcasting	29	39	35
	American Express	43	38	(12)
	A.G. Edwards	21	14	(33)
	Gulton Industries	15	8	(47)
	Hewlett–Packard	44	42	(4)
	Scientific Atlanta	23	13	(44)
	U.S. Leasing Intl.	25	23	(8)
February 18	SPS Technology	30	12	(60)
	Revco D.S.	22	30	36
	National Medical Enterprises	18	15	(17)
	Ashland Oil	30	25	(17)
	Bolt Beranek & Newman	20	15	(25)
	Criton	33	25	(24)
	Long's Drug Stores	37	30	(23)

TABLE 6–1. (continued)

Date Stock Recorded, Five Net Insider Sales	Stock	1981 Price	July 30, 1982 Price	Percentage Gain or Loss
February 25	IT&T	46	23	(50)
	Ply-Gem	7	8	14
	Schlumberger	72	36	(50)
	Tyler Corp.	23	14	(39)
	Rolm Corp.	39	25	(36)
March 4	Guardian Industries	25	15	(40)
	Pepsico	34	39	15
	Litton Industries	69	41	(41)
	M/A Comm	24	14	(42)
March 11	Harnischfeger	17	7	(59)
March 18	Continental Illinois	35	16	(54)
	McDonald's Corp.	60	73	22
	National Semiconductor	30	20	(33)
	Texas Instruments	116	89	(23)
	Veeco Instruments	18	11	(39)
	Avnet	50	40	(20)

TABLE 6–1. (continued)

Date Stock Recorded, Five Net Insider Sales	Stock	1981 Price	July 30, 1982 Price	Percentage Gain or Loss
March 25	Wal-Mart Stores	19	27	42
	TransAmerica	21	17	(19)
	Sysco Corp.	17	24	41
	Rohm & Haas	61	50	(18)
April 1	L.B. Nelson	6	2	(67)
	McDonald Douglas	45	38	(16)
	Carnation	30	33	10
	Bowne & Co.	17	9	(47)
	Mobile Home Industries	5	2	(60)

72 stocks off 23%   Dow off 16%

matched the Dow, proves that insiders can and will do better than the Dow. The 72 stocks were off 23% while the Dow suffered a 16% decline.

During the same time, there were not many multiple buys by insiders, but those that there were performed as shown in Table 6–2.

When we were out of the market in the 1970s, and early 1980s, it would have been prudent to employ money market funds, which were yielding high two-digit percentage rates. However, these rates had not been seen since the Civil War, and now, with more normal interest rates, it appears that short selling will maximize our profits when the insiders and market flash a sell signal.

Insider Action vs. Market Direction

At this juncture, notice that it is not too profitable to fight the tape. If you do, your reason must be a strong one. Notice the studies of the action of stock prices of companies with low ratings during a bull market—as a group they go up, albeit at a much lower rate than the prices of highly rated stocks. Shorting them because of insider action and ignoring market direction is no way to make money. The other side of the coin also is evident. Buying highly rated stocks in bear markets is a hard way to make money. The risk–reward factor is stacked against you.

Therefore, we bring the Insiders' Timing Formula into play. We will short at S/B 3.5 (a point over 2.5, which signifies a neutral market) when the stocks we select move *down* 5%.

When the market improves 5% and is coincident with any S/B below 2.0, then we will place stop-loss buy orders on the stocks we have sold short. Also, if the market improves 10% we will cover and cry. I suggest re-shorting if the market from this point performs as it should and moves down 5%. This ploy is a mirror image of the buying timing formula. The same principles apply to shorting and covering (buying at lower prices) that apply to buying and selling in a rising market.

TABLE 6–2. Performance of Multiple Buys by Insiders.

Date Stock Recorded, Five Net Insider Buys	Stock	1981 Price	July 30, 1982 Price	Percentage Gain or Loss
January 14	Frank's Nursery	16	13	(19)
January 21	Great A&P	5	8	60
	Pittway	4	43	8
	Cummins Engine	31	28	(10)
	Sierra Pacific Power	12	11	(8)
February 11	Clopay Corp.	8	10	25
	Rockaway Corp.	12	12	—
	Gemco National	4	3⅜	(16)
	Celanese	65	42	(35)
	First Union Realty	16	15	(6)
February 18	Bankers Trust	15	29	93
March 11	Standard Shares	39	37	(5)
March 18	AMP Inc.	49	52	6
	Avemco	9	12	33
	George A. Hormel	16	18	13
	Intercity Gas	14	7	(50)

"Portfolio" up 6%

Dow off 16%

Eleven issues out of 16 outperformed the Dow (69%).

Selling short scares most people because the potential loss is limitless, whereas in buying you can lose only the money you have advanced. The Timing Formula alleviates that feeling of the possibility of unlimited loss and should work well to give us profits no matter what the market does. If you can still feel squirmish in shorting then do so at a very high S/B, for example, 4.5 instead of 3.5.

Emotionally, people feel that selling short is negative, that one should not bet on bad performance or profit from others' misfortune. However, this is the main reason why our capitalistic system works so well—the market rewards successs and penalizes weak results. Successful companies increase shareholders' equity and are able to raise capital easily in the marketplace for continued expansion. Everyone profits—officers, labor, and stockholders.

The following example illustrates employment of the Insiders' Trading Formula in formula-declared bear markets. In previous timing illustrations, we placed our money obtained from stock sales into money market funds. However, there is no reason that stocks with low insider ratings in a bear market should not act even *worse* than the market, just as high rated stocks in a bull market can act *better* than the market.

The S/B ratio reached 3.5 in March 1976 (with the Dow at 999), so selected stocks that had low insider ratings were shorted. Not until February 1978 did the market make a subsequent *low* concurrent with an S/B of below 2. The Dow was at 743 and the S/B at 1.82. From this low, the market moved up 5% to 780 in April, and with the S/B at 1.06, stocks were bought to cover the shorts. A juicy Dow spread of 219 points yielded good profits on our shorts.

7

Analyzing Insider Buys and Sells

When an Insider Sells

As has been discussed in Chapter 4, it is easy to deduce why an insider buys the stock of his company. It is not so easy, however, to analyze why an insider sells. There are many reasons for an insider to sell. Part of his compensation is in the form of stock options, and he may need to sell stock he gets from those options for living expenses. Also, estate planners harp on the merits of diversification. Besides the high cost of living, other expenses (e.g., illness of a family member or college tuition) can generate a sell decision by the insider.

A scant handful of academic studies exist that show that insiders have an edge over outsiders in investment acumen. These studies, however, have fallen short in the number of stocks selected for study and short in the time covered. They also fall short in that they do not discriminate among trades and analyze each one, whereas according to my method of analysis, there are "good" (meaningful) insider trades and "useless" (nonindicative) ones.

Analyzing an Insider's Sells

Because we cannot introduce ourselves to every insider to ask his reasons for selling (as if we'd get the right answer anyhow!), it seems that we are stymied. Perhaps it is one reason why many analysts discount insider activity in security analysis. There *are* assumptions, however, that *can* qualify sales so that we can assume whether a sale was for investment or personal reasons. The more assumptions, the greater chance that we *can* qualify an insiders' trade and identify whether it was executed because of an investment decision on his part.

Number of Trades

The first obvious qualifier is the number of sales transacted by an insider. If he makes one isolated trade, we can assume it is not necessarily an investment decision. If an officer sells repeatedly over a period, however, he is probably making an investment decision. Also, the number of sell trades by more than one officer is all-important. If only one or two executives are selling, that can be shrugged off, but if many are selling that is a different story. The more votes, the more of a mandate is the election!

Percentage of Holdings

The next qualifier for an individual trade is percentage of holdings. If an officer sells a minute portion of the stock he holds, we can assume it is to raise pin money. However, if he lets go a high percentage of his stock, then this is another indication that the trade is for investment purposes.

Unanimity

If all of a company's insider trades are on the sell side—not a solitary contrary vote—then we can assume that these transactions are not coincidental. The odds are that the insiders are wary. Unanimity means undivided opinion. There must be some catalyst that is causing the insiders to act in unison.

Market Direction

When you analyze an insider trade, be aware of the general market direction. If an insider sells in a rising market, he believes that even the market won't bail him out. If he buys in a falling market, he is in so much of a hurry that he does not want to wait for a probable lower price. If he chairs a machine tool company and other stocks in that industry are moving up, but he sells the stock of his own company anyway, this action has extremely negative implications about his company. Software companies are exploding on the upside, but executives of Acme Software are selling. Beware!

Insider Reversals

The one insider happening that should really alert us to the fact that "something is up (down?)" is when insiders reverse. That is, they have been buying stock in their company, but they reverse and start to sell. A change of mind is tantamount to a declaration of no confidence. It means that some development has occurred to cast doubt on the company's future. WATCH OUT!

A hypothetical example: Many insiders of ABC Inc. are selling a large percentage of their holdings; not one executive is buying. The market is moving up—especially other companies in

ABC's industry. They are selling now, but seven months ago the insiders of ABC were buying. Insiders are screaming to us outsiders: "Caution, look somewhere else!"

We now know how to qualify selling and, almost without a shadow of doubt, can tell if insider selling is sporadic or for disinvestment. Selling of itself is bearish because the insider can usually raise money by means other than selling stock. If he is bullish on his company, he can borrow the money he needs by using his stock for collateral.

Do not put much emphasis on simply the number of shares the insider sells or the office he occupies. It is more important to know that a vice president has sold 5,000 shares out of 5,500 than to know that a chief executive officer has sold 10,000 shares out of 200,000. It's the percentage that counts, and the vice president could well know more about the company's prospects than the chairman—he's in the trenches!

When an Insider Buys

An insider buy is a vote of confidence, as we have said before. We must also analyze insider buys so that we can qualify the trade and grade its importance. Is it a token purchase to please stockholders? Is it an all-out plunge, or is he merely getting his toes wet? Is he a smart investor?

Analyzing an Insider's Buys

We can analyze an insider's buy by using the same reasoning that we used in analyzing sales. We can qualify them and arrive at assumptions that can serve as guides for our own actions.

Number of Trades

Each insider buy tends to confirm that all others he has made have been undertaken by the insider for good reasons.

Percentage of Holdings

If a new trade is only a small percentage of an insider's previous holdings, we can reasonably assume that the insider has less conviction of the worth of the stock than if he buys a high percentage of his previous holdings. The latter action would indicate that the insider has little doubt that his purchase will be profitable.

Unanimity

When all the officers of a company are buying, when none seems to have a negative viewpoint, we can probably assume that they have good reason to view the stock positively. A concensus is important.

Market Direction

When an officer buys in a weak market, he is discarding the thought that he can get a better price by waiting. We can put a bullish connotation on this, but we must know the direction in which the market is moving before we can arrive at the correct interpretation. Insiders' confidence is also shown if the buy involves a company in an industry segment that appears weak.

Insider Reversals

A reversal is all-important. If a company's insiders have been selling, and then they change their minds and start buying, that can be a clear signal that a change is in the wind. If they are buying, then we had better buy too, after giving a good look at the company and its stock!!

A hypothetical example: Pay especial attention to a company whose insiders are making numerous purchases, with no dissenting sells. Most insiders are doubling up their positions even though the market is going south, especially other stocks in the same industry. The insiders are buying now, but previously they were selling. If I find a company in which this scenario is unfolding, I always, somehow, find a place for it in my portfolio!

8

Rating a Stock

It is possible that you can extract from the records only those insider trades that pertain to the stocks you have an interest in. You can then base your analysis on those only. It also is not out of the question to glance at total insider activity to separate trends or items of possible interest. However, to save me and my readers hours upon hours of time, the *Vickers Weekly Insider Report* has computerized all the variables needed to examine the universe of insider trading.

The Rating Formula

To arrive at numerical readings that make sense out of the thousands of facts that have been entered into the computer and to enable us to easily find those stocks that are experiencing attractive insider activity, I have weighted those evaluators and qualifiers discussed in Chapter 7. If you are setting up your own program, you may want to arrive at your own weighting system, but I have found that awarding points to stocks by the following formula works well:

- Each sale transaction is awarded 1 minus point.
- Each buy transaction is awarded 2 plus points.

Over the years, as I have already pointed out, it can be seen that there are about two sales for every buy by insiders—everything being equal. Nothing is always equal, but the 2:1 ratio seems apropos. Therefore, I give the buy trades twice the number of points that I assign to sell trades. If an insider sells 25 to 49% of his holdings, 2 minus points are given; 50 to 74%, 3 minus points are added; 75 to 100%, 4 minus points are added.

Remember that a certain mathematical quickstep is needed to arrive at an accurate percentage of the insider's "now has" position before a trade. On the sell side, we have to add the shares sold to his "now has" position (after the trade) to arrive at the shares he held *before* the sale. On the buy side, we subtract the shares bought from his current position to arrive at the shares he held before the trade.

If an insider buys 50% more than he held before his trade (had 200 shares, buys 100 more), 6 plus points are added to his score. If an insider adds more than 100% to his previous holdings, then with each 100% 1 point is added to an original 8 points for the first 100% increase. For example, a director who had 200 shares and then buys 1,000 more now owns 1,200 shares. This is 600% of his original 200. Thus, 8 points are given for the first 100% increase and 1 point for each 100% more (5 points for the remaining 500%). A total of 13 points is awarded. A doubling of position is awarded 8 points (had 1,000; buys 1,000 more). Initial holdings are given only 4 points. This precludes a stock being awarded a mass of plus points if a handful of new directors establish their customary nominal position.

If all the trades in a particular company are sales, 4 minus points are added to each trade. If the insiders are unanimous in their buying, then 8 plus points are added to each trade.

If an insider sells into a rising market; minus 1 point is added. Two plus points are added if he buys into a falling market.

If a particular industry's stock prices are doing well, and insiders sell stock in a company that is in that industry, minus 1 point is added. Conversely, insiders buying in an industry whose prices are falling are credited with 2 plus points.

Notice that no points are awarded for size of trade. It is more important that a vice president sells 4,000 out of 5,000 shares than if a CEO sells 20,000 out of 200,000.

Also, hierarchy is given no weight. Many times a vice president of sales will know much more than an absent chairman of the board. And he might be a better investor as well.

Reversals by Insiders

The reversal phenomenon can be construed as more than an assumption. It borders on certainty.

The all-important reversal on the sell side is awarded minus 8 points. A reversal from insiders selling to insiders buying garners 16 plus points. A reversal occurs when a company's index rating changes from a plus to a minus, or vice versa. More than one trade is necessary, however. To repeat, one trade is no help in our analysis.

The stocks shown in Table 8–1 were all the buy reversals recorded in 1984—those stocks that showed a reversal from a minus (insiders' selling) to a plus rating (insiders' buying). Because the year was a washout, 1984 is a good year to study the effect of reversals by insiders. The Dow ended the year only a handful of points different from where it started. So, market action not being much of a factor, this study has more credence than if the market had moved substantially one way or the other.

Table 8–2 shows all equities in which during 1984 insiders reversed and became *sellers* after previously buying.

Table 8–3 shows all the reversals recorded in the second quarter of 1985 and at what prices the insiders sold or bought. As you can see, the insiders batted 1000%—an incredible performance.

The year of 1986 was turbulent, beginning with the Dow at 1580, and hitting 1900 twice, with a 1700 interlude in between.

Table 8–4 shows all the buy reversals during 1986. The average appreciation was 52% compared to the Dow's 36% advance—taken from the midpoint of the Dow's range in 1986 (1738). The reversals out-performed the surging Dow by a fantastic 42%. These 34 stocks appreciated 64% if sold at their 1986–1987 (October) highs. Remember Loeb? If a 10% stop-loss discipline was applied on these stocks, then a 54% gain would have realistically been achieved—compared to 49% seen by the Dow (1738 to 2596 of October 1).

The stocks shown in Table 8–5 were the first 34 *sell* reversals (insiders switched from buying to selling) in 1986. The 34 appreciated 2.8% as of September 1, 1987. The Dow appreciated 18 times what the 34 experienced.

If the 34 sell reversals were shorted on the dates listed in column one below, and then covered 10% *above* their 1987 lows seen in column six, the 34 depreciated 11%. Even in a bull market, low-rated stocks yielded a good profit. What profits

TABLE 8–1. Insiders' Buy Reversals in 1984.

Stock	Date	Price	Price on January 25, 1985
Toys 'R' Us	February 29	34½	Became Multiple Sale 9/26 @ 50
Golden West Homes	March 21	9	5⅞
Wal-Mart Stores	March 21	32	Became Multiple Sale 8/29 @ 44
Church's Fried Chicken	April 4	22	33⅞
Winkelman Stores	May 23	13	15¼
Avon Products	July 18	21½	21½
Oakwood Homes	August 8	14¾	22⅜
Houston Natural Gas	August 15	51½	44⅜
Seagull Energy	August 15	13	16½
Lomas & Nettleton Financial	September 12	22⅜	32
Financial Corp. of America	September 19	4½	10⅝
Seligman & Latz	October 17	16¼	14¼
Tultex Corp	October 24	12	13

"Portfolio" up 57 points (21%)
DJIA (from January 2, 1984 to January 25, 1984) up 0%

*Bear in mind that *most* investment managers do not equal the Dow's performance year in and year out.

81

TABLE 8–2. Insider Sale Reversals.

Stock	Date	Price	Price on January 25, 1985
Dixico	January 11	5	7⅜
Amfac	January 18	30	24⅞
Intercole	February 22	9	8⅝
Weathersford	May 23	8¼	4¼
Gulfstream Aerospace	June 27	17½	15¼
Clorox	July 23	29	28⅞
Wal-Mart Stores	August 29	41½	46⅝
Montana Power	September 12	22⅛	19⅜
Toys 'R' Us	September 26	33¼	30½
Peabody International	November 7	9⅛	8¼

"Portfolio" down 11 points (5%)

TABLE 8–3. Insiders' Reversals in 1985 (Both Buy and Sale).

Company	Reversal Date	1985 Price Range	Average Insider Sale Price	Average Insider Buy Price
Radiation Systems	April 3	8⅝–16¼	15	9
Rollins Environmental	April 3	8¼–29⅜	17	12
Sea Land	April 10	14⅝–27½	24	17
Hasbro Bradley	April 10	38½–15½	27	18
CACI Inc.	April 10	2⅝–6¼	5.17	3.82
Planning Research	April 24	8⅝–15¼	14¼	12½
Beard Oil	May 1	4¾–9¾	7	7
Dover Corp.	May 1	32¼–42½	38	35
Geo International	May 8	3¼–8	6.125	4.79
Valmont Industries	May 8	18¾–24½	22	19
American Business Products	May	20¼–27½	23	21
Bankers Trust NY	May 22	38–75⅝	65	57
Becton Dickinson	May 22	30¾–53⅞	48	40
Comdisco	May 22	8–17¼	16	12
Integrated Resources	May 22	11⅞–26⅛	18	17
Nuclear Data	May 22	6⅞–11⅞	10⅝	6⅞
Gordon Jewelry	June 5	13¾–18¼	16	16
Itel	June 12	2¾–8¾	7¾	4¾
Financial Corp., Santa Barbara	June 19	2½–6	3.93	3.71
Zenith Laboratories	June 19	4–23¼	14	5

TABLE 8-4. Buy Reversals in 1986.

Date Reversed	Stock	Price	Price on March 24, 1987	Percentage Gain or Loss	1986–October 1987 High Price
January 1	Cummins Engine	72	81	13	95
January 15	Carolina Power & Light	30	40	33	43
January 22	Wells Fargo Mortgage & Realty	24	21	(13)	30
January 22	Sea-Land Corp.	22	28 (Acquired)	27	Acquired
February 5	Firestone Tire & Rubber	24	37	54	50
February 26	Tele-Communications	20	32	60	45
March 19	Panhandle Eastern	22	33	50	34
March 26	Toys 'R' Us	26	39	50	43
April 9	Network Systems	12	17	42	19
April 16	Daisy Systems	14	10	(29)	14
April 23	Baker International	14	18	29	25
April 30	Frank B. Hall	25	14	(44)	25
	Kaufman & Broad	20	27	35	29
May 21	Libbey-Owens-Ford	18	23	30	44
June 4	Planters Bankers	17	18	6	20
June 25	Irvine Sensors	¾	1	33	1

TABLE 8-4. *(Continued)*

Date Reversed	Stock	Price	Price on March 24, 1987	Percentage Gain or Loss	1986–October 1987 High Price
July 9	FMC Corp.	18	32	78	NA
	Emulex	6	8	33	10
July 23	Planning Research	19	Became Sell Reversal	68	Became Sell Reversal
	Epsilon Data Management	5	9½	90	15
August 6	Gannett Co.	32	48	56	56
August 20	Reebok International	8	24	200	25
	Nichols Institute	8	6	(25)	10
	International Clinical Labs	14	14	—	22
August 27	Lee Data	6	8⅝	44	10
	Trans-Canada Pipelines	12	16	33	17
	J.P. Morgan	47	45	(4)	54
	Keystone International	14	20	43	24
	AVX Corp.	11	17	55	21
September 3	LSI Logic	9	16	78	21
September 24	VMX	3	4½	50	6
	Scientific System Services	2½	2⅜	(5)	4
	Cullen/Frost	18	13	(28)	18
	Amdahl	21	39	86	49

85

TABLE 8–5. Sell Reversals in 1986.

Reversed	Stock	Price	Price on September 1, 1987	Percentage of Gain or Loss	1987 Low (to September 1 Low)
January 1	Horizon Corp.	4	4½	13	4⅜
	Planters	19–26*		37	
	Sci-Med Life Systems	20	11	(45)	10
	Tandy Corp.	38	48	26	38
February 5	Towle Manufacturing	5	1	(80)	⅞
	Planning Research	15–19*		27	
	Harris Graphics	13	22 (Acquired)	69	
March 5	Continental Illinois	9	5	(44)	4½
March 12	Frank B. Hall	20–25*		20	
March 19	AM International	7	8	14	6
	Gerber Products	40	53	33	40
March 26	Medtronic	64	102	60	76
	Federal Paperboard	25	49	96	28
	Creative Computer Application	1½	⅝	(58)	⅜
April 9	Shaklee	19	25	32	18
	Epsilon Data Management	9–5*		(44)	
	Champion Enterprises	15	8	(47)	6
April 16	Sealed Power	29	37	28	26

TABLE 8–5. (continued)

Reversed	Stock	Price	Price on September 1, 1987	Percentage of Gain or Loss	1987 Low (to September 1 Low)
April 23	Toro	18	21	17	15
	Noel Industries	7	2	(71)	1½
	Cincinnati Microwave	12	6	(50)	6
	Pitney-Bowes	32	46	44	35
June 11	Interlake	41	48	17	38
	Brown & Sharpe	27	23	(15)	17
	Great Western Financial	18	21	17	18
June 25	Venturian Corp.	19	15	(21)	15
	Texas Eastern	34	38	12	27
July 16	J.P. Morgan	85–94*		11	
July 23	Benihana National	8	6	(25)	3¼
	Intelogic Trace	17	5	(71)	4½
August 6	General Homes	10	6	(40)	6
August 13	Flour Corp.	14	19	36	11
September 24	Western Digital	14	27	93	18
	Thomas Industries	20	21	5	16

"Portfolio": + 2.82%; DJIA: + 50.17%

*Became a buy reversal before September 1, 1987.

would have been seen if the shorts were executed in a bear market?

The following examples are merely illustrations to clarify and demonstrate the rating system:

Example 1:
Zurn Industries

Date	Nature of Trade	Shares	Now Has
8/4/86	S	2,503	820
8/28/86	S	100	2,081
9/11/86	S	500	1,581
10/7/86	S	1,400	181
9/24/86	S	3,505	226
9/11/86	S	2,000	6,171
10/15/86	S	6,171	–0–
9/26/86	S	1,000	1,957
10/6/86	S	1,000	957

Points	
9 sales	– 9
% of holdings	– 15
unanimous	– 36
vs. market action	– 9
Rating	– 69

Example 2:
Zweig Fund

Date	Nature of Trade	Shares	Now Has
9/25/86	B	19,531	30,227
9/25/86	B	1,500	1,500
9/25/86	B	1,400	1,400
9/25/86	B	3,000	3,000
9/25/86	B	1,000	1,000

	Points
5 buys	+ 10
% of holdings	+ 24
unanimous	+ 40
vs. market action	+ 20
Rating	+ 94

Example 3:
Clark Equipment

Date	Nature of Trade	Shares	Now Has
8/8/86	B	800	1281
8/8/86	B	400	586
9/3/86	B	200	300

	Points
3 buys	+ 6
% of holdings	+ 30
unanimous	+ 24
vs. industry	+ 6
reversal	+ 24
Rating	+ 90

Example 4:
E Systems

Date	Nature of Trade	Shares	Now Has
8/14/86	S	20,000	83,262
10/1/86	S	1,000	7,906
8/29/86	S	5,000	45,060
6/19/86	S	3,000	14,077
7/2/86	B	889	10,221
9/11/86	B	300	300
10/27/86	S	2,000	7,000

	Points
5 sales	− 5
2 buys	+ 4
% of holdings	+ 2
vs. market action	− 2
Rating	− 1

Example 5:
Fairchild Industries

Date	Nature of Trade	Shares	Now Has
6/26/86	S	2,050	N.R.*
7/29/86	B	400	4,655
7/24/86	S	10,000	96,901
7/28/86	B	9,000	113,142
9/15/86	S	2,000	N.R.*
11/15/86	S	500	500

Points	
4 sales	− 4
2 buys	+ 4
% of holdings	− 5
vs. market action	− 4
vs. industry action	+ 8
Rating	− 1

*Did *not* report.

Example 6:
ROWAN Companies

Date	Nature of Trade	Shares (cv. debs)	Now Has
7/29/86	B	840	1,000
10/27/86	B	375	3,500
6/13/86	B	250M	250M
6/13/86	B	250M	250M
6/13/86	B	250M	250M
6/13/86	B	250M	250M
10/27/86	S	4,000	109,153
6/13/86	B	2,875M	2,875M
6/13/86	B	500M	500M
9/26/86	S	2,000	3,150
10/6/86	B	3,000	5,000

Points	
2 sales −	2
9 buys +	18
% of holdings +	32
vs. industry +	18
reversal +	56
Rating +	122

Table 8–6 (see pages 94–103) illustrates the rating system in full operation. The asterisk is assigned by the computer to those stocks that have experienced the all-important insider reversal.

The rating system makes no pretentious claims to be scientific. No formula can read the insiders' minds. A report on companies with similar ratings does illustrate, however, impressive evidence of its ability to predict future price action.

Table 8–7 (see pages 104–106) shows stocks, taken alphabetically, that in January 1985 had ratings from 20 to 29. These 33 stocks appreciated 41% during the rest of the year compared to the DJIA's 29%. The 33 showed only five issues with a loss for the year. The Dow did well, but stocks with a − 20 to − 29 (see Table 8–8 on pages 107–109) appreciated less than half as much, with 13 of the 33 falling in price.

On January 2, *1986*, 23 stocks had a plus rating of 30 to 39. The group appreciated 38.1% during 1985. The biggest winners were the stocks listed in Table 8–9 (see page 110) (up 74% in 1985). Even with this advance, the group continued strong. By April 30, 1986, they increased 23% more in value compared to a 15% increase by the Dow.

TABLE 8–6. Computer-Generated Ratings.

ADT INC	−2
A L LABS INC CL A	26
APL CORP	28
ABBOTT LABS	−5
ACUSON	−16
ADAMS RUSSELL INC	20
ADAPTEC INC	−11
ADOBE RES CORP...12% PFD	20
ADOBE SYS INC	−29
ADTEC INC	−7
ADVANCED SYS INC	9
AEQUITRON MED INC	2
AETNA LIFE & CAS CO	−32
AFFILIATED BANKSHARES COLO I	20
*H F AHMANSON & CO	78
AIR MIDWEST INC	−8
ALASKA AIR GROUP INC	−6
ALBERTSONS INC	−39
ALEX BROWN FINL GROUP	11
ALEXANDERS INC	−7
ALLEGHENY & WESTN ENERGY COR	−11
ALLEN GROUP INC	−10
ALLIANCE FINL CORP	14
ALLIANT COMPUTERS SYS CORP	−11
*ALLIED BANCSHARES INC	76
ALTERNACARE INC	14
AMERADA HESS CORP	−27
AMDAHL CORP	−25
AMERICAN BARRICK RES CORP	−20
AMERICAN BLDG MAINTENANCE IN	14
AMERICAN CR CARD TEL CO	−9
AMERICAN CYANAMID CO	−18
AMERICAN FAMILY CORP	26
AMERICAN GREETINGS CORP CL A	−21
AMERICAN HEALTH PPTYS INC	26
AMERICAN MED INTL INC	4
AMERICAN NURSERY PRODS INC	−8
AMERICAN SOFTWARE INC CL A	−21
AMERICAN WESTERN CORP NEW	−6
AMES DEPT STORES INC	−22

TABLE 8-6. *(continued)*

AMERIWEST FINL CORP	20
AMP INC	−25
AMRE INC	14
ANALOG DEVICES INC	−25
ANDROS ANALYZERS INC	−23
ANHEUSER BUSCH COS INC	−15
ANITEC IMAGE TECHNOLOGY CORP	−25
ANTHONY INDS INC	32
AON CORP	8
APACHE CORP	24
APPLE COMPUTER INC	−24
APOLLO COMPUTER INC	−20
ARCHIVE CORP	−15
ARITECH CORP DEL	26
ARK RESTAURANTS CORP	−9
ARKANSAS BEST CORP	1
*ARROW ELECTRONICS	−13
ARTISTIC GREETINGS	48
ARUNDEL CORP	38
ASSOCIATED INNS & REST CO AM	30
ATLANTA GAS LT CO	26
ATTENTION MED CO	32
AUTOMATIC DATA PROCESSING	−24
AUTOMATIX INC	11
AUTOTROL CORP	17
AVATAR HOLDINGS INC	14
AVNET INC	−8
BRT RLTY TR SBI NEW	44
BNH BANCSHARES INC	44
BALDWIN & LYONS INC CL B	20
BALDWIN PIANO & ORGAN CO	−41
BALL CORP	−18
BALTIMORE GAS & ELEC CO	20
BANCTEC INC	−13
BANDAG INC	12
BANKAMERICA CORP	26
BANKERS FIRST CORP	20
BARD (C R) INC	−10
*BASIX CORP	26
BAXTER TRAVENOL LABS INC	−12

TABLE 8–6. *(continued)*

BAYBANKS INC	18
BEAUTICONTROL COSMETICS INC	36
BECTON DICKINSON & CO	−17
BEL FUSE INC	−11
BELL ATLANTIC CORP	34
BERES INDS INC	−9
BERKEY INC	−14
BEST PRODS INC	5
BETZ LABS INC	−9
BEVERLY INVT PPTYS INC	42
BIOSPHERICS INC	−13
*BIOTECHNICA INTL INC	−12
BLASIUS INDUSTRIES INC	9
BLOCKBUSTER ENTMT CORP	−11
BOISE CASCADE CORP	−19
BONNEVILLE PAC CORP	−11
BORG-WARNER CORP	−24
BOW VALLEY INDS LTD	−19
BOWNE & CO	−20
BRADY (W H) CO CL A	−17
BRIDGE COMMUNICATIONS INC	−23
BRISTOL MYERS CO	−18
BRITTON LEE	−19
BRUSH WELLMAN INC	−32
BUEHLER INTL INC	30
BUSINESSLAND INC	−13
BUTLER MFG CO DEL	−12
CEM CORP	−17
CIGNA CORP	−6
CPI CORP	−21
CNB FINL CORP KANS	18
CNW CORP	−9
CP NATIONAL CORP	−21
CABOT CORP	−31
CACI INTL INC CL A	−16
CADMUS COMMUNICATIONS CORP	−14
CADNETIX CORP	−12
CALGENE INC	−11
CALLAHAN MNG CORP	−20
*CALMAT CO	29

TABLE 8–6. *(continued)*

CALPROP CORP	−5
CAMBRIDGE BIOSCIENCE CORP	−15
CANADIAN OCCIDENTAL PETE LTD	−31
CANADIAN PAC LTD COM PAR $5	−10
CANRAD INC	−8
CANYON RES CORP	−14
CAPITAL CITIES ABC INC	−10
CAPITAL FED SV&LN ASSN CALIF	−12
CAPITAL HLDG CORP DEL	14
CAREMARK INC	−9
CARLISLE COS	−18
CAROLINA FREIGHT CORP	−11
CATERPILLAR INC	−28
CELLULAR PRODS INC	−8
CENTENNIAL GROUP INC	34
CENTOCOR INC	−18
CENTRAL FIDELITY BKS INC	−3
CENTRAL HOLDING CO	30
CENTRAL LA ELEC INC COM NEW	−3
*CENTRAL PACIFIC CORP CALIF	38
CENTRUST SVGS BK MIAMI FLA	34
CETUS CORP	−39
CHANDLER INS LTD	14
CHARMING SHOPPES	−76
CHARTER CO	−11
CHARTWELL GROUP INC	−17
CHEMED CORP	−10
CHIRON CORP	−10
CHRYSLER CORP	−39
CHURCH & DWIGHT CO	−15
CHURCHILL DOWNS INC	36
*CHURCH'S FRIED CHICKEN INC	50
CHYRON CORP	26
CINCINNATI FINL CORP	24
CIRCLE FINE ART CORP	22
CIRCLE K CORP	6
CINTAS CORP	−13
CITICORP	−62
CITIZENS FIRST BANCORP	−2
CITYFED FINL CORP	22

TABLE 8–6. *(continued)*

CLABIR CORP	−10
COATED SALES INC	−46
*COCA-COLA CO	28
COCA COLA ENTERPRISES INC	28
COLECO INDS INC	−37
COLONIAL GROUP INC CL A	−7
*COLOR SYS TECHNOLOGY COM PAR	−12
COLT INDS INC COM NEW	−21
COLUMBIA SVGS & LN ASSN CALI	−22
COMDISCO INC	−29
COMERICA INC	22
COMMERCE BANCORP INC N J	22
COMMERCE BANCSHARES INC	14
COMMERCE GROUP INC	−26
COMMERCE UNION CORP	−8
COMMERCIAL CR CO	14
COMMERCIAL FED CORP	−9
COMPAQ COMPUTER CORP	−40
COMPONENT TECHNOLOGY CORP	24
COMPREHENSIVE CARE CORP	20
CONSOLIDATED FIBRES INC	−9
CONSOLIDATED FREIGHTWAYS INC	−42
CONSOLIDATED STORES CORP	38
CONTINENTAL CORP	28
CONTROL DATA CORP DEL	−8
CONVENIENT FOOD MART INC	30
CONVEX COMPUTER CORP	−34
COORS (ADOLPH) CO CL B	−39
COPYTELE INC	−11
CORESTATES FINL CORP	4
CORNING GLASS WKS	−34
CORROON & BLACK CORP	6
CRAY RESEARCH INC	−29
CROSBY (PHILIP) ASSOC INC	−16
CROWN CRAFTS INC	3
CUTCO INDUSTRIES INC	38
DALTEX MED SCIENCES (COM&WT)	−11
DATA GEN CORP	−30
DATAPOINT CORP COM PAR $0.25	−3
DATAPRODUCTS CORP	1

TABLE 8-6. *(continued)*

DAYTON HUDSON CORP	−2
DELTONA CORP	16
DELUXE CHECK PRINTERS INC	2
*DESIGNS INC	32
DESOTO INC	−9
DEXTER CORP	−2
DIAMOND BATHURST INC	−9
DICEON ELECTRS INC	−38
DIGITAL EQUIP CORP	−97
DIGITAL COMMUNICATIONS ASSOC	−21
DISNEY (WALT) CO	−44
DIXON TICONDEROGA CO	−16
DOVER CORP	−20
DOW CHEMICAL CO	−15
DREYFUS CORP	2
DU PONT (E I) DE NEMOURS & CO	−61
DUKE PWR CO	12
DUN & BRADSTREET CORP	−32
DUQUESNE SYS INC	−31
DUPLEX PRODS INC	−17
DURAMED PHARMACEUTICALS INC	−11
DURIRON INC	−17
DYCOM INDS INC	−25
EG & G INC	−16
ELXSI LTD	−8
E M C CORP MASS	−14
E M C CORP	−22
E-SYSTEMS INC COM PAR $1	21
E Z EM INC	−20
EAGLE PICHER INDS INC	−19
*EASTERN GAS & FUEL ASSOCIATE	44
EASTOVER CORP SBI	−2
EATON CORP	−16
*ECOLOGY & ENVIRONMENT INC CL	−11
EL CHICO CORP NEW	12
ELCOR CORP	−12
EMERALD HOMES L P DEP RCPT	40
EMHART CORP (VA)	20
ENTRE COMPUTER CTRS INC	−17
ENVIRONMENTAL DIAGNOSTICS IN	−12

TABLE 8-6. (continued)

ENVIRODYNE INDS INC	−21
EVANS & SUTHERLAND COPMPUTER	−9
EXCEL INDS INC	−16
EXPEDITORS INTL WASH (COM&WT	−17
FNW BANCORP INC	22
FACET ENTERPRISES INC	2
FAIRCHILD INDS INC	−5
*FAIRFIELD COMMUNITIES INC	60
FANSTEEL INC DEL	−19
FARAH INC	−13
FEDERAL EXPRESS CORP	−26
FEDERAL MOGUL CORP	−7
FEDERAL PAPER BRD INC	−14
FEDERATED DEPT STORES INC	−29
FINANCIAL BENEFIT GROUP	14
FINANCIAL CORP SANTA BARBARA	3
FIRESTONE TIRE & RUBR CO	−22
FIRST BANC SECS	22
FIRST CENT FINL CORP	86
FIRST CHICAGO CORP	−1
FIRST CITY BANCORPORATION TE	−20
FIRST FID BANCORPORATION	−11
FIRST ILLINOIS CORP	38
FIRST LIBERTY FINL CORP	18
FIRST MICHIGAN CAP CORP	18
FIRST MIDWEST BANCORP INC DE	18
FIRST MISSISSIPPI CORP	−6
FIRST PENNSYLVANIA CORP	20
FIRST PEOPLES FINL CORP	−5
FIRST SEC CORP KY	14
FIRST UNION CORP	−10
FIRST WISCONSIN CORP	27
FIRSTIER FINL INC	19
FISHER SCIENTIFIC GROUP INC	70
FLEET FINL GROUP INC	32
FLEMING COS INC	−21
FLIGHT DYNAMICS INC	−17
FLOATING POINT SYS INC	−11
FLORIDA PROGRESS CORP	34
FLORIDA ROCK INDS INC	−22

TABLE 8–6. *(continued)*

FLORIDA STEEL CORP	-21
FLOWERS INDS INC	-17
FLUKE (JOHN) MFG CO INC	-14
FORD MTR CO DEL	-48
FOREST OIL CORP	-11
FOREST OIL CORP CL B	-14
FOSTER WHEELER CORP	-20
FOURTH FINANCIAL CORP	28
FREEPORT MCMORAN INC	-16
FREMONT GEN CORP	-9
FRUIT OF THE LOOM INC CL A	22
*GAF CORP	74
GCA CORP	-2
GABELLI EQUITY TR INC	62
GALOOB (LEWIS) TOYS INC	-36
GALVESTON HOUSTON CO	15
GAP INC	-25
GATEWAY BANCORP INC	13
GATEWAY COMMUNICATIONS COM N	-9
GENCORP INC	-10
GENERAL CERAMICS INC	-1
GENERAL DYNAMICS CORP	-41
GENERAL HOMES CORP	-38
GENERAL INSTRUMENT CORP	-7
GENERAL MTRS CORP	-71
GENETICS INST INC	-14
GENTEX CORP	-9
GENRAD INC	-16
GENUINE PARTS CO	20
GEODYNE RES INC	-29
GEO INTERNATIONAL CORP	-24
GENZYME CORP	-26
GEORGIA GULF CORP	3
GEORGIA PACIFIC CORP	-35
GILLETTE CO	-29
GLOBAL MARINE INC	-16
GOLDEN VY MICROWAVE FOODS IN	-23
GOULD INC	26
GRACE (W R) & CO	-20
GRANDVIEW RES INC	-10

TABLE 8–6. *(continued)*

GRANGES EXPL LTD	−17
GRAPHIC INDS	14
GREAT ATLANTIC & PAC TEA INC	−32
GREAT FALLS BANCORP	18
GREENWICH PHARMACEUTICALS IN	−9
GROUNDWATER TECHNOLOGY INC	−42
GRUBB & ELLIS CO	−4
GRUEN MKTG CORP	20
GUARDSMAN CHEMICALS INC	40
GUILFORD MILLS INC	4
GULF & WESTERN INC	−9
HRE PPTYS	32
HADCO CORP	−14
HALL (FRANK B) & CO	44
HALLIBURTON CO	−22
HANA BIOLOGICS INC	−7
HARKEN OIL & GAS INC	20
HARPER INTL INC	20
HAWKEYE BANCORPORATION	20
HEALTHCARE INTL INC CL A	−15
HEALTHVEST S B I	36
HEALTHDYNE INC	24
HELIX TECHNOLOGY CORP	−15
HELMERICH & PAYNE INC	−34
HEMOTEC INC	30
HERSHEY OIL CORP	7
HEWLETT-PACKARD CO	−15
HIBERNIA CORP CL A	−1
HILTON HOTELS CORP	−11
HOLIDAY CORP	42
HOLMES (D H) LTD	−9
HOMAC INC	14
HOME INTENSIVE CARE INC	−15
HONEYWELL INC	−24
HORIZON AIR INDS INC	34
HORIZON BANCORP N J	20
HOSPITAL CORP AMER	−11
HOWELL INDS INC	−14
HOWTEK INC	−23
HUDSON GENERAL CORP	−13

TABLE 8–6. *(continued)*

HUMANA INC	−30
I C H CORP	14
IC INDS INC	−9
I M S INTL INC	1
I R E FINL CORP (COM NEW)	34
ICOT CORP	−13
IMMUNEX CORP	−17
IMO DELAVAL INC	34
IMPERIAL CORP OF AMERICA	30
IMATRON INC	−8
INCO LTD (COM)	−26
INDIAN HEAD BANKS INC	−1
INERTIA DYNAMICS CORP	−16
INFORMIX CORP	−30
INFOTRON SYS CORP	−8
INFORMATION RESOURCES INC	−15
INNOVEX INC	−9
INSITUFORM NORTH AMER INC CL	2
INSTRON CORP	−18
INTELLIGENT SYS MASTER L P	−3
INTEL CORP	−43
INTER REGL FINL GROUP INC	42
INTERCO INC	−1
INTERGROUP CORP	18
INTERLEAF INC	−27
INTERMET CORP	−34
INTL BUSINESS MACHS CORP	−26
IOMEGA CORP	−9
IPCO CORP	−10
JB'S RESTAURANTS INC	−4
J P M INDS INC	44
JAMES RIVER CORP VA	−27
JAMESWAY CORP	−19
JAVELIN INTL LTD	26
JEFFERSON-PILOT CORP	18
JERRICO INC	−37
JOHNSON & JOHNSON	−16
JOULE INC	34
JUNO LTG INC	−18
K D I CORP	32

TABLE 8–7. *Stocks with a Plus (Insider Buying) Rating of 20 to 29.*

Company	Price on January 2, 1985	Price on December 31, 1985	Percentage of Appreciation or Loss
American Ecology	7	20¼	189
Banks of Iowa	42	56½	35
R.G. Barry	4⅛	5½	33
Bell Atlantic	80⅜	106½	33
Castle & Cook	13	13⅛	1
Champion Spark	8¼	9⅝	17
Columbia Gas	34	39½	16
Comdisco	11⅛	28⅝	157
Compaq Computer	7	14½	107
Computercraft	4¼	1¼	(71)
Danaher Corp.	7	7⅞	13
Datum Inc.	5½	5½	0
Empire Airlines	7½	14⅝	95
Ensearch	21	22¼	6
Fairmont Financial	7¼	20	176

TABLE 8–7. (continued)

Company	Price on January 2, 1985	Price on December 31, 1985	Percentage of Appreciation or Loss
GAF Corp.	24½	59	141
Gelco Corp.	16¾	19¾	18
Genrad	15⅜	13⅛	(15)
Genstar	24¼	27⅞	15
GEO Intl.	3⅜	2	(41)
Grubb & Ellis	8	9¾	22
Hannaford Bros.	13⅞	26⅝	92
Hasbro Bradley	21¾	34¾	60
Mapco Inc.	26⅛	38	46
Material Sciences	10⅝	15¼	44
Micropolis Corp.	5¾	8¾	52
Montana Power	19¼	32⅜	68
Planning Research	13¾	16⅛	18
SL Industries	10¼	13	27
Shopwell Inc.	9⅜	9	(4)

TABLE 8–7. (continued)

Company	Price on January 2, 1985	Price on December 31, 1985	Percentage of Appreciation or Loss
Thomas & Betts	35⅞	40¾	15
U.S. Steel	26⅛	26⅝	2
Victoria Bankshares	22¾	20¾	(9)
			+41%

TABLE 8–8. Stocks with a Minus (Insider Selling) Rating of 20 to 29.

Company	*Price on January 2, 1985*	*Price on December 31, 1985*	*Percentage of Gain or Loss*
Aceto Chemical	15⅞	17⅜	16
Amer. Cyanamid	50	57½	15
Amer. Maize-Prods.	13¾	12⅜	(10)
Amer. Surgery	2	½	(75)
AMP Inc.	33⅜	36	9
Archer–Daniels	19⅛	26	36
Arvin Inds.	14¾	21⅞	48
Atlantic Richfield	44⅛	63¾	44
Automatic Data	39	59	51
BDM International	13½	25	85
BR Communication	11	7⅞	(28)
Basix Corp.	10⅜	10⅛	(2)
Bell Fuse Inc.	10¼	6	(42)
Beverly Enterpr.	31½	36⅜	15
Big V Supermarket	11⅛	16	44

TABLE 8–8. *(continued)*

Company	Price on January 2, 1985	Price on December 31, 1985	Percentage of Gain or Loss
Biogen	5½	14⅝	166
CP National	19	27¼	43
Cagles	7⅞	7½	(5)
Can Occidental	19¼	18¼	(5)
Centex	23⅞	25⅜	6
Charter Medical	22⅝	21⅜	(6)
Chesebrough-Ponds	33⅝	42⅜	26
Citicorp	38⅝	49⅜	28
Clorox Co.	28¾	47⅝	66
Coachman Inds.	17⅜	13⅜	(23)
Coherent Inds.	19½	16¾	(14)
Collins Foods	10	13¾	38
Computervision	37¼	12⅝	(66)
Control Data	35¼	20¾	(41)
Dayton-Hudson	31⅝	45⅞	45

TABLE 8–8. *(continued)*

Company	Price on January 2, 1985	Price on December 31, 1985	Percentage of Gain or Loss
Deere & Co.	29¾	28¾	(4)
R.R. Donnelley	49	63⅝	30
Dunkin' Donuts	15⅝	23	47
			+ 16.6%

TABLE 8–9. *The Big Winners in 1985.*

Company	Percentage Gain in 1985	Price on January 1, 1986	Index Rating on January 15, 1986	Price on April 30, 1986
American Integrity	73	22½	+36	28
Bell Atlantic	33	53¼	+30	63¾
Cincinnati Gas & Electric	50	22⅛	+38	24½
Durkon Industries	77	13⅜	+33	13⅛
Itel Corp.	86	9¾	+32	13½
Medtronic Inc.	61	43½	+35	66
Noel Industries	105	5⅛	+36	8
Weingarten Realty	353	19⅞	+34	20½
Wetterau	57	39⅛	+31	39½

9

Dow +6%, Insiders +68%, and Other Data

Table 9–1 (see pages 112 and 113) is comprised of all those stocks rated +50 or higher on January 2, 1985. Index data go back six months, so each stock was arbitrarily priced at its 1984 low, again on August 31, 1985 (before a bull market upleg began), and then six months later on February 25, 1986, which happened to be an all-time market high.

Analysis of the performance of these stocks helps to answer two paramount questions:

1. Are the insiders good investors?
2. What lead time do the insiders seem to have over market action?

TABLE 9-1. Stocks Rated +50 or Higher: January 2, 1985.

Stock	84 Low	Price on August 31, 1985	Percentage Gained from 1984 Low	Price on February 25, 1986	Percentage Gained from 1984 Low
American Hoist & Derick	7½	12⅛	+62	10	+33
Applied Circuit Technology	¾	1⅝	+116	1⅜	+83
AZP Group	14½	24⅜	+68	27⅝	+91
BMC Industrials	10¼	8¾	-15	3⅝	-65
CACI Inc	2⅝	3⅞	+48	2⅞	+10
DBA Systems	7	16½	+136	14	+100
Dataproducts Corp.	13⅜	12½	-7	15⅞	+19
Dillard Department Stores	10¼	32½	+217	38⅜	+274
Walt Disney Productions	45¼	89⅜	+98	129	+185
Entex Energy	16⅜	16⅝	0	10⅞	-34
Esselte Business Systems	12⅝	22⅝	+79	30	+138
Fortune Financial	12½	21¾	+74	24	+92
Fur Vault	3⅝	11½	+217	13¼	+266
Galaxy Oil	1½	1⅞	-25	⅝	-59
Great American First	8⅛	17⅞	+120	28¼	+248

Stock	*84 Low*	*Price on August 31, 1985*	*Percentage Gained from 1984 Low*	*Price on February 25, 1986*	*Percentage Gained from 1984 Low*
Integrated Resources	11⅞	19½	+ 65	35⅛	+196
Interlake	41	47⅝	+ 16	58¼	+ 42
Itel Corp.	2⅜	8⅛	+242	10	+363
Kalvar Corp.	⅝	⅞	+ 40	1⅛	+ 80
Korea Fund	12	14¼	+ 19	23¼	+ 94
Laidlaw Industrials	9	17⅛	+ 90	17⅝	+ 96
Minstar Inc.	10½	23	+119	23	+119
NERCO Inc.	10	12½	+ 25	11⅞	+ 19
Nortek Inc.	12	16⅝	+ 39	19⅜	+ 62
PSA Inc.	15	26	+ 73	27½	+ 83
Sci-Med Systems	5	9	+ 80	12¾	+155
Sea-Land Corp.	14⅝	21	+ 44	21¾	+ 49
Silicon General	6¼	6¼	0	3¾	− 40
Storage Technology	2	2⅛	+ 6	3⅜	+ 69
Valmont Industrials	16¼	17⅜	+ 7	15½	− 5
Wilfred American Educational	8	12¼	+ 53	12⅝	+ 58
Appreciation			70%		88%

Notice that stocks not acting well in the first period did even worse in the second—with one exception. This underscores the maxim: Cut your losses short. They only multiply.

The Dow industrials appreciated 6% from January 1, 1984 to August 31, 1985. Those stocks that were rated +50 or higher by our index appreciated 70%. This provides a conclusively affirmative answer to the first question. The answer to the second question seems to be implicit in the fact that these stocks appreciated 68% in about a year (the base prices occurred at different dates in 1984). In the following six months, these stocks appreciated only 20% from their August 31 prices, whereas the DJIA was up 26%. Of the 31 stocks, 22 showed greater appreciation by August 31, 1985 than they showed from that date to February 25, 1986. Thus, it seems that the insiders can "see" about a year into the future.

Any portfolio or managed list of stocks would be hard pressed to match the meteoric rise in the stock market for the first quarter of 1987. However, the insiders accomplished this feat, as borne out by Table 9–2 (see pages 116 and 117). This list was unmanaged, except that each stock commanded a +60 or higher insider rating during the first quarter of the previous year—1986. These highly rated companies appreciated on average 54.3% from the average price paid by the insiders to April 22, 1987. The Dow appreciated only 51% during this time.

Insiders tend to act too quickly (particularly Texans), and the seven oil-patch stocks brought down the end result in dramatic fashion. Without energy-related issues, the +60 stocks would have shown a hefty 71% appreciation. The seven did start to make a substantial move later on. If the stocks had been sold at their 1986 to 1987 highs they would have appreciated 92%. It is interesting that in the list the 13 stocks selling at $6 or less appreciated an average 123%.

The stocks listed in Table 9–2 were *all* New York Stock Exchange stocks that were rated within the 10 highest (i.e., in insiders' buying) throughout 1985. As a group, they would have appreciated 109% if they had been sold at their 1986 highs. This, of course, would have been impossible, but if the insiders' formula had been used, the appreciation would have still reached 95%. For a formula almost to match the highest prices 25 stocks achieved over two years is hard to believe, but the proof is shown in Table 9–3 (see pages 118 and 119).

The stocks listed in Table 9–3 were not selected; they comprised all the stocks listed in the "Top Ten" category, however. It is possible that the individual investor could have bested this result by employing good selection, especially if on October 3 he had had the opportunity to rebuy, to reshuffle, or to discard.

The stocks shown in Table 9–4 (see pages 120) were all the stocks rated in the "Top Ten" during January and February 1986. They appreciated 30% when they were sold by formula the following June 30—six months later. The S&P 500 moved from 211 to 247 for a gain of only 17%.

I have repeatedly said in this book that insider buying is more important to us outsiders than is their selling. There is only one reason for an insider to buy on the open market. Verily, there are several economic reasons why he should *not* buy: He can obtain cheap stock by means of corporate options. If he wishes to diversify, he can do so by buying stocks other than those of his own company. As I have mentioned many times, there are many noninvestment reasons for him to sell.

Table 9–5 (see pages 121 and 122) lists stocks that were all among the "Top Ten" in the last half of 1986. They more than participated in the soaring market of 1987.

The "Top Ten" of the last six months of 1986 appreciated 48%. The Dow has appreciated 35% thus far in 1987. The 21 top-rated stocks did 37% better than did the Dow. Remember: These stocks were not chosen. They were all the listed stocks in the "Top Ten" category. You would have done much better by eliminating some and doubling up others(!?)

We have just discussed the superlative performance of top-rated stocks. The "least-liked" 10 that were tallied at the same time—January and February 1986—and that were sold when the insiders flashed a sell signal in May showed depreciation by the end of 1986, as can be seen in Table 9–6 (see pages 123 and 124). This table shows that it *is* important to tally insider selling as well as buying. Fourteen out of the 19 stocks depreciated. The average stock's price was off 11.7%, whereas the Dow was up 6%.

In September 1986 a bombshell concerning flat earnings was dropped by Hospital Corporation of America. Wall Street

115

TABLE 9–2. *Stocks Rated + 60 During First Quarter, 1986.*

	Average Insider Price	Price on January 2, 1987	High in 1986–1987	Price on April 22, 1987	Percentage of Gain to April 22, 1987
Aileen Inc.	2⅝	4⅜	5¾	4⅞	86
American Fructose	5½	13	17	12	118
BASIX Corp.	7¼	7	12	8	(10)
Broadview Financial	2¼	2⅜	5½	3¼	44
Cityfed Financial	12	12	18	10	(17)
First City Banc (TX)	11½	3	14	7	(39)
Golden West Financial	35	35	47	37	6
Harken Oil & Gas	1	2½	4¾	4	300
Helson Industries	2	2⅛	3⅝	3	50
Hotel Properties	17½	Acquired @ 23			31
Intelogic Trace	8¾	6⅝	18	6⅝	(24)
LLC Corp.	1⅛	Acquired @ 5¼			366
Lone Star Technology	8½	6¼	15	12	41
Union Exploration Partners	19	16	20	19	—
Windmere Corp.	4	6¾	10	10	150
Advanced Telecommunications	6	10	19	19	217

TABLE 9–2. (continued)

	Average Insider Price	Price on January 2, 1987	High in 1986–1987	Price on April 22, 1987	Percentage of Gain to April 22, 1987
International Controls	25¼	24	36	26	3
Ensearch Exploration	17	13	19	17	—
Union Corp.	6⅛	8⅝	13	10	63
Tektronix Inc.	26	39	43	34	31
Valley National Corp.	39	42	50	37	(5)
Toro Co.	17	32	33	31	88
Market Facts	10	10	14	9	(10)
Riverside Group	5	13	13	13	160
Northern Telecom	26	41	46	44	69
First Continental REIT	6	3¼	6⅝	3⅜	(44)
United Bankers	7½	5	9	5½	(27)
American Physicians Service Group	3¼	3⅝	5¼	3⅝	12
Clevetrust Realty Investment	16½	14	19	12	(21)
Phillips Petroleum	12½	16	17	16	28
CCX Corp.	4⅜	4½	5½	4⅜	—
R.G. Barry Corp.	5¼	6⅞	10	9	71

TABLE 9–3. Proof of the Pudding.

Date Listed	Stock	Price When Listed	Sold in 1986 by Formula	Re-Bought by Formula	1986–1987 High	Price on July 26, 1987	Total Percentage of Gain*
January 2, 1985	Nerco	11	12	10	23	22	118
	Esselte Business Systems	15	34	32	46	45	213
	PSA (PS Group)	21	29	32	38	34	47
	Integrated Resources	14	30	25	31	30	150
January 16	American Hoist & Derrick	8	9	8	12	10	38
	Comdisco	10	21	17	33	30	240
	CSX Corp.	25	33	29	38	37	64
February 13	Pacific Resources	7	16	16	17	15	114
27	Pantry Pride (Revlon)	5	17	13	20	20	380
	American Capital Bond Fund	19	24	25	25	21	5
April 10	Great American First Savings	11	15	18	25	17	27
17	Textron	22	29	30	40	39	73
May 1	Portland General Electric	18	30	32	37	25	28
22	WMS Industries	5	10	6	8	8	140
June 12	Bowater	21	29	29	43	36	71
July 10	First City Bancorp	11	9	5	14	13	46
August 7	United Stockyards	8	9	9	12	9	13
21	Diversified Energies	23	28	25	27	24	17

TABLE 9–3. (continued)

Date Listed	Stock	Price When Listed	Sold in 1986 by Formula	Re-Bought by Formula	1986–1987 High	Price on July 26, 1987	Total Percentage of Gain*
September 18	Enron	41	42	40	51	47	22
	Bell Atlantic	44	69	67	77	66	55
October 12	U.S. West	36	53	55	62	51	36
9	Insilco	17	23	22	26	24	47
16	Union Exploration Partners	23	17	16	21	21	(4)
23	LLC Corp.	1	5	5	5	5	400
December 11	BASIX	8	11	7	11	6	25
	Average stock up						+95%

*Columns 3 plus 8.

TABLE 9–4. The "Top Ten," January–February 1986.

Company	Prices on January 2, 1986	Prices on June 30, 1986	$100 Invested in Each Stock on January 2, 1986
CityFed Financial	12	18	$150
Lone Star Steel	9	9	100
Union Exploration Partners	19	16	84
LLC Corp.	2	4	200
First City Bancorp/TX	13	8	62
Windmere	5	6	120
Intelogic Trace	11	16	146
Hotel Properties	19	22	116
BASIX Corp.	10	11	110
International Controls	31	30	97
Heldor Industries	2	3	150
Harken Oil & Gas	1	1½	150
Market Facts	10	14	140
Riverside Group	5	9	180

$1400 invested became $1805 or +30% for 6 months—60% annualized.

TABLE 9–5. The "Top Ten," Last Half of 1986.

	Listed Among the "Top Ten"	Price	Price on August 20, 1987	Percentage of Gain or Loss
July 2	Northern Telecom	14	24	71
	R.G. Barry	5	8	60
	Phillips Petroleum	10	18	80
	CCX	4½	5	11
	Kenner Parker Toys	23	49	113
	Kelly Oil	10	11	10
July 9	FMC Corp.	21	49	133
	Lukens Inc.	14	50	257
July 16	Rowan Companies	4	10	150
July 23	BRT Realty Trust	15	19	27
August 20	Pandick	17	Leveraged Buy Out (LBO) @ 27	59
September 3	Black & Decker Corp.	15	26	73
September 10	Conston Corp.	14	9	(36)
September 17	Mountain Medical Equipment	4⅝	5	3
November 5	Equimark Corp.	5	4	(20)
	Leslie Fay	18	10	(44)

TABLE 9–5. (continued)

	Listed Among the *"Top Ten"*	*Price*	*Price on August 20, 1987*	*Percentage of Gain or Loss*
November 12	American Capital Management & Research	18	18	—
December 17	Reliance Group	10	11	10
	Germany Fund	9	12	33
December 24	Zweig Fund	10	10	—
	Health-Chem	9	10	11
		Average appreciation:		48%

TABLE 9–6. Depreciation of "Least-Liked" Stocks (Low Insider Ratings).

Company	Prices on May 27, 1986*	Prices on December 31, 1986	Percentage of Gain or Loss
Motorola	46	36	(22)
NCR	56	44	(21)
Coleco	20	8	(60)
Federal Express	64	63	2
Hilton Hotels	74	67	(10)
Citicorp	63	53	(16)
United Technologies	50	46	(8)
Charming Shoppes	22	20	9
American Greetings	37	26	(30)
McDonald's Corp.	48	61	27
Gillette Co.	43	49	14
Gibson Greetings	25	16	(36)

TABLE 9–6. (continued)

Company	Prices on May 27, 1986*	Prices on December 31, 1986	Percentage of Gain or Loss
IBM	147	120	(18)
Bridge Communications	14	15	7
Ford Motor	53	56	6
General Motors	78	66	(15)
Browning–Ferris	37	45	22
Phibro–Salomon	55	38	(31)
TRW	106	85	(20)

*When insiders gave the sell signal.

was shocked. The stock fell 7¾ points the next day. HCA had a low index rating of minus 95 on August 27.

From July 18, 1986, 10 insiders had sold 101,413 shares. There was no insider buying.

Other stocks in the hospital industry were also hit hard. American Medical International, which dropped 4 points, had a low rating of minus 33. National Medical Enterprises, down 2⅜, had a rating of minus 25. Humana, with a minus 36 rating, lost 3 points. Beverly Enterprises had a rating of minus 25 and was down 3¼.

It should be noted at this juncture that insider activity can be "read." Certain companies, for one reason or another, always seem to have a great many insider sales. It is recognition of *extraordinary* selling that is important, and after studying insiders for a time, you can easily ascertain activity that is out of the ordinary. You must learn to detect activity out of the norm because it can foretell either future good news or disappointments. One example of this could be seen in the activity—or rather, inactivity—of International Paper. In the last half of 1985, 13 insiders sold IP. In the first quarter of 1986, there was only one sale, and International Paper stock moved from 47 to 116.

Another good example of insiders decreasing their selling pace was Wal-Mart. This retailer garnered very negative insider ratings from 1984 through the first half of 1986, as a result of the stock's meteoric price increase coupled with a generous officers' option plan. During September 1986 the market underwent a 200-plus point slide, and the price of Wal-Mart was sliced some 25%. From a high negative insider rating, Wal-Mart went into plus territory—insiders bought! The stock rapidly recovered and appreciated over 30 points to a new high.

I have commented on the fact that Dow blue chips see a good deal of insider selling. Two examples of out-of-the-ordinary selling are important.

From March through July 1986, there was more insider selling of IBM than at any other period. Twenty-nine officers sold 144,043 shares.

The following letters were exchanged at this time between myself and IBM:

IBM Insider Trades*

July 22, 1986

The July 16 Heard on the Street referred to stock trading activity by IBM officers.

Unfortunately, misunderstanding of stock transactions by company officers and directors frequently results from reports sold by stock monitoring services. Many of these services provide incomplete information since they mention only stock sales, but ignore the other half of the equation which is acquisition of stock. Information on both is publicly available through the Securities and Exchange Commission.

We would like to state the facts in IBM's case to remove any confusion or misrepresentation. In the nine months between October 1985 and June 1986, 29 IBM officers and directors sold 144,043 shares of IBM stock. During the same period, 41 IBM officers and directors acquired 173,981 shares.

James C. Reilly
Director of Communications
International Business Machines Corp.
Armonk, N.Y.

**Reprinted by permission of the *Wall Street Journal*.*

August 14, 1986

IBM writes a letter to the editor (July 22) saying that insiders had both sold and "acquired" shares of IBM.

From SEC documents, it is apparent that the last time IBM insiders bought shares in the open market was August 1985 and that all of the acquisitions since have been by exercising options.

Generally this is not a bullish indicator because of the "discount" that is obtainable in option prices. IBM insiders acquired up to four new shares by surrendering one share of stock they held. Therefore, the Heard on the Street column by Linda Sandler (July 16), taking note of IBM insider selling prior to publication of disappointing earnings, was entirely justified and IBM's reply strictly semantic.

Edwin A. Buck
Editor
Vickers Weekly Insider Report
Brookside, N.J.

In the first half of 1986, 43 General Motors officers sold 95,616 shares of GM stock. The company commanded the lowest insider rating of any company in our experience. Both GM and IBM subsequently reported lower than expected earnings and predicted tougher sledding ahead. The prices of the stocks were slashed.

It would seem that by using statistics to arrive at a conclusion of what a person or persons is thinking is an abnormality—as scientific as alchemy.

The process certainly is not foolproof; however, the insiders' rating techniques prove that we are, at least, on the right track. The preceding chapter offers studies sufficient in number to validate our rating formulae.

We have harnessed insider thinking and can turn it into a valuable analytical tool, indispensable for arriving at investment decisions.

10

Companies in Trouble

Insiders' Call Turnarounds

When a company goes "bottoms up" and suffers great misfortune, what does the investor do? Without intimate knowledge of the company's operation, the outsider cannot ascertain if the current adversities are permanent or merely a temporary jolt. Does the investor price-average by buying more stock? If there can be some confirmation that all is not lost, the troubled company's stock can be a great buy.

Again, we can profit by seeing what the insiders do. Insiders are good bargain traders. They are buyers when they believe their knowledge indicates that the market is wrong—or that they can eventually prove it wrong. The *Business Week Letter* printed a study that showed that if in 1960 the 100 equities with the worst performance had been listed and concurrently the 10 with the heaviest insider buying had been bought, and if the resulting income from those investments had been reinvested in a like manner each year through 1968, the portfolio would have shown a 400% appreciation by January 1, 1972. During the same period, the S&P 500 appreciated 50%.

A watch list of companies that are suffering reduced earnings and fallen stock prices should be kept by prudent investors—if at the same time the stock of those companies is being bought by those companies' executives.

Each of the companies listed in Table 10–1 reported a loss in 1985. Each had a plus Insiders' Index Rating for the fourth quarter of 1985. By the end of 1986, the average stock had appreciated 69% compared to the DJIA's 29% for the year. Not bad for a bunch of "losers."

Chapter XI

When a company appears to be headed for insolvency, it files Chapter XI of the bankruptcy laws. This gives it protection from creditors for a time so that it can take steps to solve its problems internally. This is official adversity! Its stock continues to trade (and is footnoted VJ in the stock tables). Here again insiders can alert us to those companies that might emerge successfully from Chapter XI status. There are many examples of companies that have successfully avoided full bankruptcy and that have rewarded stockholders. Some well-known examples and now highly profitable companies are Penn Central, Chicago Milwaukee, GEICO, United Merchants, FM Manufacturing, Wickes, and Pantry Pride (now Revlon). Each of these companies had insider buying transactions during and after their reorganizations.

TABLE 10-1. *Companies with Losses in 1985.*

	Price on December 31, 1985	1986 High	Percentage of Gain or Loss
A.M. International (+32)	6	$8\frac{3}{8}$	44
Algorex (+19)	$7\frac{7}{8}$	$8\frac{3}{4}$	11
Anacomp (+16)	$3\frac{3}{8}$	$6\frac{5}{8}$	96
Astrotech Int'l (+42)	$1\frac{1}{8}$	$3\frac{1}{8}$	178
Centronics (+44)	5	$8\frac{1}{4}$	65
Deltona Corp. (+15)	$7\frac{1}{8}$	$10\frac{1}{4}$	44
Dynascan (+14)	7	$14\frac{3}{8}$	105
Fairchild Industries (+15)	$10\frac{3}{4}$	14	23
Genisco Tech (+28)	$5\frac{3}{4}$	$7\frac{1}{8}$	24
GEO International (+34)	$3\frac{3}{8}$	4	19
MSI Data (+26)	$10\frac{1}{8}$	$14\frac{3}{8}$	42
L.E. Myers (+56)	$2\frac{3}{8}$	$8\frac{1}{4}$	247
NCA Corp. (+12)	$3\frac{7}{8}$	$6\frac{1}{2}$	68
Noel Industries (+36)	$5\frac{1}{8}$	$10\frac{3}{4}$	110
Oakhill Sportswear (+16)	$3\frac{7}{8}$	$10\frac{3}{4}$	177

TABLE 10-1. *(continued)*

	Price on December 31, 1985	1986 High	Percentage of Gain or Loss
Pope Evans & Robbins (+26)	3½	4⅛	18
Present Co. (+22)	7	11⅜	63
Purolator Courier (+27)	23¾	28⅞	22
RMS Electronics (+24)	4⅞	1¾	(64)
Robbins & Meyers (+10)	12½	13¾	10
Roper Corp. (+58)	8	21¼	166
Sierracin (+12)	6¾	8⅞	32
Williams Electronic (+20)	6¼	12¼	96
	163.25		Average 69%

An investor's own inclinations can be adhered to. There are degrees of misfortune: from a most precarious position of bankruptcy to a state of temporary setback. The risk–reward factor can be brought into play as suits the investor.

Most investors prefer not to play bankruptcies. In fact, it should be left to the professional. A good example of limited risk and potential substantial rewards is Black & Decker, Inc. This company over the years has performed well and could be classified as a pale blue chip, having dominated its limited niche—home power tools. The company all of a sudden had new management, an expensive purchase of General Electric's Kitchen Appliance Division (a bite almost as big as itself), a restructuring of its manufacturing plants, and lower foreign sales as a result of a high-priced dollar. All this was too much at one time, and earnings fell. The stock went from $26 in 1985 to $14.50 in the fall of 1986—while the bull market raged.

At almost the absolute low of 15, seven insiders stepped in and purchased 75,000 shares in July and August of 1986. It seemed like a perfect low-risk adversity situation because the insiders by their actions were showing confidence that a turnaround could be expected. The stock now sells at $26.

R. G. Barry, in an ailing footwear industry, suffered a loss of $0.25 per share for 1985. During the year, management disposed of nonprofitable divisions and factories. Operational start-up costs in Mexico also penalized earnings. There was a good deal of insider buying in the first half of 1986. The stock commanded a plus 66 rating by June. From a low of $4 in 1985, the stock recently sold above $10.

11
Studies by Industry

Insider breakdown by industry is interesting—not only to focus in on those industries where action might be had but to see how individual companies are doing vis-à-vis their counterparts. I use the computer to arrive at Insider Index Ratings by industry. This information is useful in isolating industries that are showing unusual buying or selling by comparing their index numbers with the insider universe. The goal is to isolate those companies that will perhaps outperform their peers. If a company has a positive rating compared to negative ratings of other companies in the same industry, we can deduce that, if we like the industry, this outfit bears investigation.

135

An interesting observation is the close relationship between bank insider trading and the all-important interest rate. Banks realize higher earnings when interest rates are falling; conversely, rising interest rates translate into falling earnings. The reason for this is that banks cannot abruptly change their customers' interest rates. Thus, the cost borne by them for funds increases faster than what they can charge. Their yield margin is squeezed when interest rates are rising.

From the point of the highest interest rates in 1980 right through 1986, banks' S/B ratio was the lowest of any industry, which signified intense insider buying. The prime rate currently is one-third of its 1980 record.

In September 1986, the market suffered a quick sharp loss of 200 Dow points. Many analysts blamed this on a sluggish bond market that was signalling the prospect of higher interest rates. "Not so," I wrote. Bank insiders were buying at such a clip as to cause the industry's insider index to rise from a plus 0.88 to a plus 2.65 as against a negative 8.05 for all stocks. Bank insiders do not buy in the face of rising interest rates. The 200-point dip was soon erased as the market raced on to new highs.

When Wall Street was bullish on oil stocks in the 1970s, and while the prices of those stocks were booming, the industry's insiders were selling to such an extent it could have been called a wholesale bailout. Of course, the insiders were right. The oil glut slowly developed, and oil stocks were slashed in value. Conversely, insiders called for better petroleum prices as early as April 1986. The industry insider index moved to a plus 4.19 compared to the overall market's average of minus 12.79. The newly formed drilling and exploration spinoffs commanded high ratings. Ensearch Exploration, plus 66; Union Exploration, plus 66; and Entex Energy Development, plus 22 are examples. By spring of 1987, many oil stocks were selling at double the 1986 lows.

We mentioned in a previous chapter the warning that the index gave us on the stocks of medical support companies that quickly dropped in favor and in price. However, one stock, Medtronic, had a plus 35 rating, in vast contrast to the medical

TABLE 11-1. Utilities with Plus Ratings, 1985.

	Index Rating	1985 Low Price	1986–1987 High Price	Price on June 30, 1987*
Carolina Power & Light	+23	24	43	34
Cincinnati Gas & Electric	+38	13	30	27
CP National	+11	18	35	31
Central Hudson G&E	+ 4	23	40	27
Houston Industries	+10	21	39	33
Portland Electric	+24	16	37	26

*The stocks listed in this table are currently selling at substantial discounts from their highs because the current market is in another period of being phobic about inflation.

industry's rating. Medtronics sold at $43 on January 1, 1986 and sells at $108 today.

Electric utilities are generally considered conservative stocks that show slow, albeit steady, growth. Perhaps this is one reason the industry usually has a lower Insider Index Rating than does the general market. As a matter of fact, the decade of the 1970s produced two villains for the industry—high interest rates and runaway nuclear energy costs. These combined to cause the electric utility index rating to be abnormally low.

However, the electric utility stocks shown in Table 11–1 are *all* those that showed plus index ratings in December 1985. Their stock action has been far better than the industry average or the general market.

12

The New-Issue Market

A profitable sector for investing is the new-issue market in which companies that heretofore were privately owned "go public" to sell stock to raise capital and to create a liquid market for their stock. Initial public offerings (IPOs) often consist of insiders' stock if officers decide not to dilute the common stock by issuing newly registered shares. Somehow a supply has to be furnished for distribution. This should not be construed as bearish if the insiders retain a good percentage of their holdings.

If, however, corporate executives sell in the aftermarket, it is not a good sign for investors. The underwriters for one reason or another have priced the stock at an attractive bailout price. Alternatively, if insiders buy in the aftermarket, it is a positive sign that the issue was attractively priced for those who know the company best (and possibly for us).

Initial public offerings can be a good market indicator. Usually at market tops there is a plethora of new-issue offerings. The offerings usually consist of a goodly amount of insiders' stock. The new issues are generally priced too high, and there are so many that they flood the market and cause an oversupply of stock, which in turn causes the whole market to weaken.

When the market correctly reflects realistic values, and new issues are attractively priced, insiders are prone to buy stock along with the public. When initial public offerings are being bought by insiders, this is a good indication that the market is healthy.

The first scenario (an unhealthy market) was beautifully unfolded in the late 1960s to early 1970s. Three or four new issues emerging a day was not uncommon. There was almost always a slew of insiders selling and at ridiculous P/Es. Calm voices compared this to the Dutch tulip mania of the sixteenth century! But momentum kept this ridiculousness going for over a year—only to be followed by a dozen years of a weak market.

After the present Big Bull market began in August 1982, it still took some time for new issues to be offered again. As this book is being written, insiders are buying their companies' new stock at a rate not previously seen by me. Scores of IPOs have been bought by insiders in the aftermarket in the past two years. One week in the fall of 1986 six IPOs were rated in my "Top Ten."

In the biggest IPO up to that date—the Henley Group—15 insiders bought 127,960 shares in the first month of the aftermarket. And this was on top of very generous options awarded these officers at the spinoff from Allied Signal plus a resolution to set aside 5,000,000 shares for officers priced at market value. Recently, Henley announced that it believes the market does not adequately reflect the company's value, so directors have voted to buy in and retire 10,000,000 shares.

There has been a good deal of insider buying of two large offerings of closed-end mutual funds—the Zweig Fund and the Gabelli Equity Trust—after the public offerings, even by Martin Zweig and Mario Gabelli. Such purchases are a vote of confidence not only for themselves but for the market.

13

The Insiders' Portfolio

On October 6, 1986, a new portfolio was born, although it is a theoretical creation on paper. This portfolio is my suggested holdings based on insider activity. October 6 was the inauguration date because the insiders flashed a buy signal on that day. Table 13–1 (see pages 144 and 145) is a history of the Insiders' Portfolio, as of its first anniversary.

A criticism of the Insiders' Portfolio might be that it includes so few issues. However, this makes it possible for the individual to participate. Other market commentators add companies willy-nilly and end up with 30 to 50 stocks. You have to be more

TABLE 13-1. Insiders' Portfolio—Results as of October 5, 1987.

Stock	Shares	Purchase		Current		Gains/(Loss)
		Dates	Price	Price	Value	
Black & Decker	300	10/03/87	16 ⅛	Sold 8/06/87 @ 25		$2,573
Henley Group	200	10/03/86	19 ½	30	$6,000	
Pandick Inc.	300	10/03/86	15 ½	Sold 1/06/87 @ 25 ⅜		$2,873
Comprehensive Care	300	10/03/86	14 ½	Sold 11/11/86 @ 13 ½		(390)
Northern Telecom	200	10/10/86	28 ¾	Sold 3/27/87 @ 43		$2,790
Black & Decker	200	10/20/86	17 ⅜	Sold 8/06/87 @ 25		$1,464
Morgan Keegan	400	10/20/86	12	12 ⅛	$4,850	
Wal-Mart	300	10/20/86	43 ½	Sold 1/29/87 @ 49 ½		$1,710
American Cap Management & Research	400	11/28/86	20 ¾	16 ¾	$6,700	
GLENFED	300	1/12/87	25 ¼	27 ⅛	$8,138	
Union Exploration Partners	600	2/05/87	17 ⅜	19 ¼	$11,550	
BRT Realty	200	2/12/87	17 ⅜	18 ¾	$3,750	
American Cap Management & Research	200	3/31/87	18	16 ¾	$3,350	
GLENFED	200	3/31/87	27 ⅝	27 ⅛	$5,425	
GLENFED	200	4/22/87	27 ½	27 ⅛	$5,425	
Laidlaw Transportation "B"	450	4/27/87	14	16 ⅛	$7,256	

TABLE 13–1. *(Continued)*

| | | Purchase | | Current | | |
Stock	Shares	Dates	Price	Price	Value	Gains/(Loss)
BRT Realty	300	6/02/87	18 ½	18 ¾	$5,625	
Henley Group	300	6/08/87	24 ¾	30	$9,000	
Fisher Scientific	500	6/22/87	14	20 ¼	$10,125	
Pier I Imports	500	9/14/87	13	12	$6,000	
Wheelabrator	500	9/17/87	19	24 ¾	$12,375	
				Total	$105,569	
				*Net Worth	$72,419 (+ 44.8%)	

*Net worth includes margin debt and interest, brokers' fees and dividends.

145

knowledgeable than your adviser as to which of these selected stocks you will invest in. Because only $50,000 was theoretically originally invested and no further funds are to be injected, the Insiders' Portfolio consists of 10 stocks.

Without the safety (and mediocrity) of diversification, we rely on the insiders to give us a green light and then employ objective and subjective rejection to come up with a few picks with outstanding possibilities. The reason funds consistently fall short of the popular market indexes is that they virtually buy the market. They are subject to too many surprises and uncertainties, and too many of them come up with a poor performance.

I also believe that the Insiders' Timing Formula will be an immeasurable asset and will help this theoretical portfolio to far outperform the market. In its brief history so far, it has outperformed the Dow by means of stock selection only. Timing has not been a factor yet because there has been no sell signal since May 1986. The Timing Formula has kept us in the market and prevented a premature exit. Also, when that rare event of more insiders *buying* than *selling* occurred in early June 1987, the portfolio took on margin to leverage its results.

As of October 5, 1987, the Insiders' Portfolio has surpassed the gain seen by five of the best acting funds* (over the last five years) by 22%.

Some explanations of why I chose particular stocks for the Insiders' Portfolio follow.

Black & Decker

Insiders bought Black & Decker near the stock's low and gave the company an index rating of plus 62. The company reported earnings of $0.46 per share for the first nine months of fiscal 1986 vs. $0.72 a year before. This was after 1985 earnings had fallen to $0.92 from $1.95 the year before. This dismal performance brought a change of chief operating officers and a

---

*Fidelity Magellan, Loomis Sayles Capital, Fidelity Destiny, Phoenix Growth, and Manhattan Fund.

subsequent management shake-up. The quarterly dividend was cut to $0.10 from $0.16. Other specifics of my choice were the following:

- Keeping an eye on insider activity.
- Recognizing the ability of the new management (which came from Beatrice Foods).
- Seeing that the assimilation of the G.E. kitchen products division was smooth and successful.
- Believing that the weakening dollar should materially help because the company's foreign sales are 44% of the total.

Black & Decker was the first stock placed in our portfolio at 16⅛.

On July 17, 1987, the company reported that fiscal third-quarter net income soared to $9 million from $604,000 a year earlier. Chairman Nolan D. Archibald attributed the growth to cost cutting and a 12% increase in sales. Half of the increase he attributed to favorable foreign exchange rates. The stock soon sold at $26.

The Henley Group

The second acquisition was the Henley Group—a creation brought about by a spin-off amounting to $3 billion of Allied-Signal assets. New start-up operations, spin-offs, or reorganizations accompanied by insider buying often present exceptional opportunities for successful investing. Quantum leaps were seen by Seagull Energy, Toys R' Us, Mediq, Weingarten Realty, and many others.

The insider buying in Henley was in addition to the receiving by these same officers of 419,510 shares from Allied-Signal. The highly regarded former president of Signal, Michael Dingman, received 323,576 shares for assuming the chairmanship of Henley.

Twenty years ago the fad was to form conglomerates. Synergy meant one plus one equals three. Now, management recognizes that concentration of effort and the discovery of hidden (conglomeratized) assets by investors is much more profitable. Thus, one plus one equals three has been replaced by four divided by two equals three.

When a Henley officer was asked: "When will you report quarterly earnings and dividends?" the answer was "We don't plan to report quarterly earnings or to have a fixed dividend rate. Our job will be to magnify value—by buying, improving, then selling, spinning off. We will not be subject to the quarterly performance syndrome." That is a very refreshing attitude that should show up in a handsome P/E ratio. We bought at $19.50.

An initial move of the company to have assets recognized was the 20% spin-off to shareholders of Fisher Scientific Group Inc. Fisher commenced trading at $14 with no price diminution of Henley stock. When Wall Street realized the size and market penetration of Fisher's products, the stock soon hit $22.

Henley then announced that it had filed a prospectus with the SEC in order to sell a sizeable but minority holding of Wheelabrator Technologies, which is Henley's waste-to-energy, cogeneration subsidiary. As happened to Henley and Fisher officers, Wheelabrator executives are to receive a generous stock purchase plan. Parenthetically, lightning struck twice; Wheelabrator was placed in the Insiders' Portfolio at the public underwriting for $19.00 and now sells at over $23.00.

Pandick Inc.

Pandick Inc. was chosen because it is a leader in the field of financial printing and should certainly benefit from an exploding stock market that is accompanied by a spate of reorganizations, mergers, and leveraged buy-outs that necessitate lengthy registration statements and proxies. Accompanied by lower earnings, the stock became a plus 62 on the index.

The fact that two weeks later the stock became a leveraged insider buy-out at almost twice our cost only bears out the efficacy of following the insiders.

Northern Telecom Ltd.

Northern Telecom Ltd. first appeared in my "Top Ten" on March 5, 1986, with a rating of plus 90. The stock was another good example of the contrarian tendency of informed insiders. The stock had not participated in the bull market (it sold as high as 41⅛ in 1985). And with good reason. The final quarter was marked by a weak earnings performance—$1.00 per share (Canadian) as against $0.99 a year before. This interrupted a growth trend in which earnings rose at a nearly 30% annual rate during the preceding four years. After announcement of the 1985 earnings, the stock fell 12 points.

The earnings for the first half of 1986 suffered because of the following:

1. Abatement of demand stemming from a switchover from analog to digital central switching and PBX systems; the company found that they had nearly saturated the market.
2. A slowing down of equipment shipments for equal access that was dictated by the divestiture of AT&T.
3. Increased R&D expenditures, especially for the business office systems division.

The company expected a strong second half, however, as well as a respectable gain in earnings for the year, based on a strengthening of orders from the Bell operating companies. Efforts in R&D undertaken during 1984–1985 have led to new products now in production. The company also anticipated good results from its transmission division, which in the recent past has been a drag on earnings.

The falling dollar should also help keep the company competitive because 80% of its manufacturing facilities are in the United States. Additionally, the Canadian dollar remains historically low in value.

In 1986 the stock of Northern Telecom sold at nine times earnings and paid out only 3% in dividends; AT&T sold at 18 times earnings and paid out 85% in dividends.

Northern Telecom reported earnings of $0.79 for the second half of 1986 vs. $0.24 the year before. In the first half of 1987 there was an increase of 26% over the first half of 1986. These earnings reflect a later two-for-one stock split. In 1987 the price of the stock rose to $46 perhaps because of expectations that the company, jointly with Martin Marietta, could land a $4.5 billion U.S. government contract. At this point, with a 50% profit, I entered a tight stop ($43), which was executed.

The company's rapid turnaround surprised me. Investigating insider activity does lead to pleasant surprises.

Morgan Keegan

There is more insider selling in brokerage firms than there is in any other business. It must be the nature of the beast. Any brokerage firm that has a high index rating, therefore, must have something going for it. However, what better industry to invest in? Share volume records are being broken every other day! Morgan Keegan is an aggressive, well-capitalized, and profitable firm operating in the Southeast, which is still the fastest growing quadrant in the country. The stock was purchased for the Insiders' Portfolio on October 20 at $12.

Wal-Mart

A meteoric stock often is accompanied by insider selling when the founders cash in and are rewarded for their entrepreneurial success. Such a stock is Wal-Mart. The company, based in the Southeast, is a high-performing retailer.

The general market "collapsed" in September 1986—especially the high-growth sector. Wal-Mart suffered a 30% decline fairly quickly. But the company, which previously always had commanded a high negative insider index rating, actually nudged into plus territory. Although there was not a torrent of buying, the selling dried up. This constituted a mandatory buy for the Insiders' Portfolio, and the stock was bought October 20, 1986, at 43½. The company participated nicely in the late 1986–1987 bull onrush, so we sold it at 49½. The high 33 P/E ratio was too high for this contrarian, and apparently the company's insiders thought so, too. Wal-Mart reappeared on our ten least-liked list.

Wal-Mart was a practical example of two insider actions that help investors:

1. When insiders reverse their actions, then they believe that either a change in results can be anticipated, or
2. They believe that the market is not levying the right value on their stock. Either way, this proved out, and the Insiders' Portfolio extracted an annualized 55% gain.

American Capital Management & Research

American Capital Management & Research was a partial spin-off from Primerica in 1986 at $23 per share, with Primerica retaining about 75% ownership. The fund appeared to satisfy all the investment objectives of the Insiders' Portfolio.

The fund manages and distributes 20 open-end and three closed-end investment funds. By December 1985, $10.6 billion was under management. This compared with $5.2 billion the year before and $18.5 billion by the end of the second quarter of 1987.

Management fees of $39,372,000 and commissions of $48,473,000 for 1985 compared very favorably with $24,159,000 and $18,512,000 in 1984. The third-quarter 1986 figures alone were $15,439,000 for management fees and $11,893,000 in commissions. Earnings of $1.10 per share in 1985 compared favorably to 1984's $0.45. In 1986 $1.53 per share was reported.

The fund industry probably is the fastest growing in the country at the present time and shows no signs of abatement. Computer programs and "Boeskys" could enhance this growth. I expect interest rates to fall further, and this will auger well for ACM&R's fast-selling government securities fund and other high-yield funds. The company recently has added highly popular international funds to their list of products and engaged the high-sailing A. L. Williams' Insurance Company salesforce to peddle three new funds.

In April 1986, four insiders bought 31,000 shares at 22¾ to 23½. Since then, seven other insiders have bought 9,900 shares from 19⅝ to 15. Buying by insiders on the downside gives us added confidence in the company.

GLENFED, Inc.

GLENFED Inc., is the fifth largest S&L in the nation. Offices are in California and Florida, loan volume has grown 70% during fiscal 1985–1987, and savings deposits have grown 44% (well above the industry average). In 1985 earnings were $2.44 a share; in 1986 they hit $3.56. GLENFED's common stock is highly leveraged with a $1 billion FHLB advance. Other short-term debt and long-term obligations amount to $1.9 billion.

Many S&Ls in the past two decades were fatal or near-fatal casualties of high interest rates, which led to negative yield margins (i.e., their cost of money exceeded what they could charge their customers) and the flight of deposits from disintermediation (i.e., customers withdrew deposits to reinvest in higher yielding vehicles such as money market funds).

Current lower interest rates, the abundance of money, and adjustable rate mortgages (at last report GLENFED had over 90%

of its outstanding paper in adjustable rates) will translate into safer and more profitable operations for GLENFED.

The industry, even profitable operations, still sells at only five times earnings—only about 25% of the general market. This ridiculously low P/E, coupled with an excellent increase in earnings and a plus 24 insiders' rating, caused me to invest more in GLENFED than in any other position. The Insiders' Portfolio is being rewarded. The company reported earnings of $6.02 per share for fiscal 1987, and the stock is moving smartly ahead.

Union Exploration Partners

Partially to thwart the greenmailers á la Pickens, several oil companies took their exploration and production facilities and folded them into trust partnerships. Total cash flow payout to the partners resulted in elimination of income taxes for the parent company and major tax breaks for the partners because a substantial part of the payout is return of capital (which is nontaxable even with the 1986 tax reforms). Notwithstanding the plunge in oil prices, half a dozen of these partnerships were among the most heavily bought companies by partnership insiders.

Union Exploration Partners was a creation of Unocal—the sixth largest U.S. oil company. The company's production cost is among the lowest—about $4 a barrel. Reserves equal 11 years of current production. This is important because the payout of all cash flow necessitates either active exploration or plentiful reserves so that the partners' interests are not entirely depleted by extraction of the resource.

The partnership began trading at $24, before the precipitous drop in oil prices to below $9 a barrel. Twelve insiders bought 137,800 shares in the aftermarket. As the price of oil collapsed, only four officers reversed to sell a portion of their stockholdings.

The recent meetings held by OPEC to stabilize prices seem to have been successful. The organization's target of $18 a barrel has been reached and seems to be holding, even exceeded.

Because both the U.S. and European economies are improving, we have probably seen the lowest prices for oil. Union Exploration trust certificates yielded 10.9% to partners in 1986. The double-barrelled attraction of a nontaxable high yield and higher earnings bodes well for the stock.

BRT Realty

BRT Realty was among my "Top Ten" highest insider ratings in July 1986 and again in January 1987. Equity was a healthy $10.08 per share, and earnings showed improvement of over 35% in 1985 and 1986. Increased lines of credit and entry into the low-cost commercial paper market will support increased loans at lower cost. In late 1986, seven insiders purchased 26,569 shares; there were no sales. Insiders now own over 50% of the stock.

In the spring and summer of 1987, all interest-sensitive stocks weakened in price. American Capital Management suffered a price setback and erosion of money under management. BRT, Morgan Keegan, and GLENFED also retreated. Fears of inflation and a still lower dollar caused Wall Street to fear that natural and Federal Reserve pressure would increase interest rates. The dread of a return to double-digit interest rates translated into mass selling of interest-sensitive stocks.

However, the insiders of banks, finance companies, and mutual funds continued their buying. Because of this insider buying, and because these stocks are selling at extremely low P/E's while earnings are on an upswing, I find myself violating a rule: "Don't fight the tape." Again, nothing is set in concrete! Fear of higher interest rates stalled the market in 1985 and 1986. However, insiders then too were buying financial stocks, interest rates remained level, and the bull market resumed.

Fisher Scientific Group

Fisher Scientific Group was added to the Insiders' Portfolio on June 23, 1987. Fisher is a health and scientific products company engaged in the design, manufacture, and distribution of laboratory equipment, apparatus, chemicals, and glassware. It also is a producer of supplies for the diagnosis of disease and for hospital therapy and infusion systems for the regulation and control of intravenous solutions.

The company became publicly owned when the Henley Group distributed 20% of the stock to its stockholders, retaining the other 80%. Because Fisher's business requires heavy expenditures for research and distribution, Henley forwarded Fisher $33 million, and Fisher obtained a $100 million line of credit from three banks. The total assets are $538,894,000 and stockholders' equity is $7.50 per share.

Because of reorganization write-offs and the acquisition of Warner Lambert's IMED Corporation, historical earnings of Fisher are almost meaningless. For 1986, the company reported a loss of $6.42 per share. First-quarter figures are indicative of what the insiders saw when they bought their stock (see Table 13–2 on page 156).

Contrary/Adversity Investing

Throughout this book there has emerged a philosophy of investing that resembles a technique known as *contrarian selection*. This method of selecting stocks involves buying unpopular issues, stocks that for one reason or another are out of public (institutional?) favor. Most investors invest in companies and industries that are on a roll, those that have earnings and prospects that look sparkling and unlimited. However, the market is a great discounter. Many times the favorable prospects are fully or overly discounted by a prescient market. When this is the case,

TABLE 13–2. Insider Purchases at Fisher.

Insider Activity		Three Months Ending March 31	
		1987	1986
Five officers bought 953,000 shares between April 22 and May 5 at prices ranging from 13¼ to 15¼ to make total holdings 1,000,000 shares.	Sales	$220,165,000	$174,414,000
	Income (Loss)	8,290,000	(3,024,000)
	Per share	$0.12	NM

the market responds sharply on the downside to any new adverse development, whether internal or external.

Most stocks in the Insiders' Portfolio have a negative factor(s) that has made the stocks unpopular or unknown—and cheap. Insiders who should know tell us that the bad news is fully discounted and that from now on the way looks up.

A very salivating situation occurs when a heretofore blue chip has stumbled. Insiders' buying notifies us that the damage has been repaired (we agree from the side), but the market is not looking because it is chasing the stars. This is our chance to buy the stock of the blue chip at a bargain price before the market at large realizes that the company is on the road to recovery.

Along with contrarian investing is adversity investing: The more the risk, the greater the reward. By following the insiders, however, we pare the risk and reap the reward.

Epilogue

It is my hope that this book has proved that analyzed insider activity, which up to now has been barely touched by practical and thorough study, can be of great help in investing, both in selection and timing.

Now you, the reader, can make this discipline even more effective by lobbying your elected officials for better and faster insider reporting. Because of the scandals recently uncovered in Wall Street involving persons who were privy to inside information, Washington might legislate harm to our free and efficient equity markets. With a little nudge from the investing public, however, perhaps the lawmakers will increase the value of our studies and at the same time cut down on illegal insider trading by speeding up and expanding the reporting required of insiders.

Presently insiders have to file their activity by the tenth of the month *following* the trade date. As a result, this invaluable information sometimes is too late to be of maximum help in arriving at a timely S/B rating. Form 4 should be filed coincident with the trade. Stockholders are in actuality the employers of all corporate officers. We should know what our employees are doing. It's just good business.

The more timely any information is, the more valuable it is. The benefits construed by our formulas and the indexing of insider activity would be tremendously increased by speeding up the reporting requirement. If insiders were compelled to report their trades *at the time of the trades,* we could have this important information six weeks earlier than is now the case.

The very magnitude of the number of Forms 4 that are (or should be) filed precludes the SEC from effectively policing their timely and effective filing. A minority (but still a large number) of insiders realize this, and if they do file a Form 4, it is often inaccurate, late, or even impossible to read. This situation could be remedied by legislation. In 1985 Senator Chafee introduced a bill (S–1382) that called for prompt (concurrent with the trade) and accurate filing, or the imposition of a fine of $50,000. If this bill were enacted into law, the SEC would surely receive better filings from corporate America. Such action would result in a fairer market for the small investor, which is something everyone today is yelling about but not doing anything about.

The current fury about a handful of bad apples—Dennis Levine, Ivan Boesky, et al.—is a slur on the great majority of corporate insiders who adhere to the law. The transgressors are outsiders with insider information that the normal course of business requires their having. These transgressors are privy to insider information.

If the SEC and the politicians are seriously trying to stamp out illegal insider activity, then they should make all such privileged outsiders file Form 4. Prosecution of violators would be easier (members of the Mafia have been convicted because of the evasion of income taxes—not for the real crimes they committed). Fewer violations would magnify the value of insider information to us investors. We could then rely with more security on that information, knowing better the attitudes of outside, but close, brokers and lawyers. There would be more knowledgeable votes for us to analyze.

It is my contention that curtailing the activity of insiders hurts the market, thus hurting the investing public. Dissemination of news regarding insiders' activity is needed, not curtailment.

An interesting episode occurred in the summer of 1986. Colt Industries proposed an offer to shareholders that caused the stock to open 29 points higher than its previous closing price. A letter appeared in the *Wall Street Journal* praising the company's executives because the stock had not moved the previous week. The stock also had been underperforming the general market for some time. The volume for Colt from July 1 to 18 was 1,345,900 shares. What about the multitude of sellers who with no warning suddenly realized that they were out $29 per share? A market that should have been discounting positive news was thwarted. Is that fair or equitable?

Nine officers at Colt sold 252,781 shares in February and March. No shares were sold by officers after that. Why did the selling completely dry up? There was nothing unethical about that. However, was their "nonaction" completely fair?

No, the law is wrong from most standpoints, and many innocent investors have suffered because of it. As Winston Churchill said about democracy: "It's a terrible form of government, but none better has been devised by the mind of man." An efficient free market might have some blemishes—but none better has been achieved by the mind of man. Any tampering by edicts that cannot be enforced is a tragedy.

Readers who agree that the market should not be tampered with but believe that public reports should be expedited and expanded should write the three legislators that are taking the lead in threatening insider regulatory changes:

- Senator Donald Riegle
  U.S. Senate Building
  Washington, DC 20510
- Senator William Proxmire
  U.S. Senate Building
  Washington, DC 20510
- Representative John Dingell
  House of Representatives
  Washington, DC 20510

Your own senators and representatives would appreciate your thoughts on deregulation.

Where to Get the Information

The following are sources of information on insider activity. The sequence is in genetical order:

- *Official Summary of Insider Transactions.* 12 issues per year. Government Printing Office, Superintendent of Documents, Washington, DC 20402. $59.00 per year. Phone: 202–783–3232.

This monthly contains every transaction; it is a replete compilation of every Form 4 filed with the SEC. As a result, each issue can be a few inches thick and contain a mass of irrelevant information. Another disadvantage is that the information is so late. Several months often go by before the insiders' transactions appear in the Official Summary.

- *Vickers Weekly Insider Report.* 51 issues per year. Vickers Stock Research, P.O. Box 59, Brookside, NJ 07926. $137.00 per year. Phone: 201–539–1336.

Brief COMMENTARY on the market or insider studies or company reports. Every open market trade of 500 shares or more is listed, as well as those traded on the OTC market. Every stock is rated by formula. Industry ratings and corporate treasury acquisitions are included. Each issue includes a chart of S/B ratio vs. the Dow Industrials and the "Top Ten" rated issues as well as the 10 "least liked" by insiders. A running, dollar-fixed suggested portfolio is presented every week.

- *Zweig Security Screen.* 12 issues per year. Zweig Securities Advisory Service, Inc., P.O. Box 5345, New York, NY 10150. $125 per year. Phone: 212-644-0040.

Twenty-three variables calculated for each stock from Performance Rating to the next date earnings per share are due as well as the number of insider transactions during the last 1, 3, and 6 months. Betas are awarded in this publication for each stock.

- *The Insiders' Chronicle.* 50 issues per year. P.O. Box 272977 Boca Raton, FL 33427. $325 per year. Phone: 305–394-3404.

All inclusive, with an in-depth featured company write-up and references to other companies. Offers a sell/buy ratio.

- *The Insiders.* 24 issues per year. Institute for Econometric Research, 3471 No. Federal Highway, Fort Lauderdale, FL 33306. $100.00 per year. Phone: 305-563-9000

Commentaries on market. Rates stocks on 1–10 basis. Rates industries. Offers insider barometers, insider buy favorites, and a lengthy suggested portfolio. The data are not all-inclusive.

The following services offer modem/personal computer on-line systems:
- *FCI—Invest/Net.* 99 NW 183rd Street, North Miami, FL 33139. Offers Form 4 information by company, date, and filer. $300 per month for 10 hours. Additional hours at $20.00 each.

- *Vickers Stock Research Corp.* 226 New York Ave., Huntington, NY 11743. Menu includes Form 4, Form 144, 13D Schedule, plus institutional portfolios and changes, traders telephone numbers, and names. Access can be had by issuer, date, filer, or broker. $50 per year hookup fee, plus $1 per minute of use.

Index

M

Major Market Index, 20
Market, new-issue, 139-141
Market direction, as per insider
   buys, 75. *See also* "Insider
   buys..."
Market direction, as per insider
   sales, 73. *See also* "Insider
   sales..."
Market trends, participation in,
   61-64
Martin Marietta, 150
Matrix, 62
McDonald's, 62
Mediq, 147
Medtronic, 136
Merrill Lynch, 24
MMM, 16, 55, 56
Mobil Oil, 59
Money-market funds, 37
Morgan Keegan, 150
Multiple sales, stocks with, as
   used by insiders, 63-67

N

NASDAQ, 35
National Medical Enterprises,
   125
New-issue market, *see* "Market,
   new-issue."
New-issue offerings, 140-141
Northern Telecom Ltd., 149-150
Not fighting the tape, 54-55
Nurock, Bob, 23
NYSE Composite, 20

O

October Massacres, 17
Offerings, new-issue, *see* "New-
   issue offerings."
Official Summary of Insider
   Transactions, 162
Oil-patch stocks, 114
OPEC, 3, 153
Option plans, effect of on S/B,
   24-25
OTC market system, 35
Owens-Corning, 62

P

P/E ratio, 148, 151, 154
Pandick Inc., 148-149
Pantry Pride, 130
Patience, 15
Penn Central, 130
Pepsico, 62
Pfizer, 55, 57
Philip Morris, 55, 58
Points, assigning, 79
Polaroid, 59
Portfolio, Insiders', 143-157
Price-averaging, 129
Price:earnings ratio, *xiii*
Prime Computer, 59
Primerica, 151
Profit sharing plans, 25
Profits, in a bear market, 61-70
Profits, protection of, 34-35
Proxmire, Senator William, 162
Prudential Bache, 24
Putnam, 23